First Days in College

DEVOTIONS TO START YOU
ON THE RIGHT COURSE.

First Days in College

Mary Harwell Sayler

BROADMAN
& HOLMAN
PUBLISHERS

Nashville, Tennessee

4253-69
ISBN: 0-80-54-5369-5

Dewey Decimal Classification: 242
Subject Heading: College freshmen/Prayer books/Devotions
Library of Congress Card Catalog Number: 93-48375

PRINTED IN THE UNITED STATES OF AMERICA

Scripture quotations marked (KJV) are from the *King James Authorized Version;* (NIV) from the Holy Bible, *New International Version,* copyright © 1973, 1978, 1984 International Bible Society, used by permission of Zondervan Bible Publishers; (NRSV) from the *New Revised Standard Version,* copyright © 1989 by the Division of Christian Education of the National Council of the Churches of Christ in the United States of America; (TEV) from The Bible in Today's English Version (also known as *Good News Bible)*—Old Testament copyright © American Bible Society 1976; New Testament copyright © American Bible Society, 1966, 1971, 1976.

Library of Congress Cataloging-in-Publication Data
Sayler, Mary Harwell.
        First days in college : devotions to start you on the right course / Mary H. Sayler.
        p. cm.
        ISBN 0-8054-05369-5
        1. College freshmen—Prayer-books and devotions—English.
2. Devotional calendars. 3. Spiritual life—Christianity.
1. Title.
BV4850.S318   1994
242'.634—dc20

                                                                93-48375
                                                                CIP

To God's co-workers
who most inspired the *First Days* series:

my son, Adam,
whose college days
coincide with this book
and
my editor and friend
Janis Whipple—

Thanks and love to both of you
for bringing me joy,
for showing dauntless faith and good humor,
and for helping me to remember
what God wants me to do.

INTRODUCTION

As you head for college, take along the translation of the Bible you most like to read! Modern scholarship provides many accurate and highly readable versions from which you can choose, such as *The Amplified Bible, The New Jerusalem Bible, New American Bible, New American Standard, New King James Version, Revised English Bible,* or *New Century Version.*

In this devotional book, Scripture has been taken from the translations frequently used in church worship services and Bible studies by Christians of all denominations. These versions of the Bible are shown as follows:

KJV   *King James Authorized Version* of the Bible approved by James I of England who reigned from 1603 to 1625.

NIV   Holy Bible, *New International Version.*

NRSV   *New Revised Standard Version* Bible.

TEV   The Bible in Today's English Version (also known as *Good News Bible)*

By becoming familiar with various translations, you can select the version that speaks deeply, directly, and most clearly to you. If you can't decide, look for an edition that features two or more translations side by side on each page. Or get to know them all, and become a Bible scholar!

For additional help, many publishers add study notes which can be very beneficial. Done well, study notes provide information about Bible history or culture and clarify word choices in translating the biblical text. However, some notes are merely opinions which may differ from yours. So, keep in mind that footnotes are not the Word of God but the Bible is! Let God's Word speak to you in a translation you easily hear.

This is what the Lord says—
your Redeemer,
the Holy One of Israel:
"I am the Lord your God,
who teaches you
what is best for you,
who directs you
in the way you should go."
(Isa. 48:17, NIV)

Congratulations on the arrival of your special day! For months—maybe years—you've thought about going to college, and the day has finally come for that wonderful adventure!

Selecting a school might have been an easy decision for you to make. If not, you're probably having extra doubts right now! That's to be expected. But even if you knew from grade school which college you would choose, you still had time to wonder, "What if *they* don't choose *me?*"

Waiting for an acceptance letter gave time to agonize over your SAT score, final exams, and grade point average. But, thank God, the letter did arrive! Now you've packed your favorite Bible with your other valuables. You've updated your address book, found flip-flops for showering, and bought enough underwear to keep you from having to do the laundry for at least three or four weeks. You're ready! You're on your way!

As you say good-bye to family and friends, don't be surprised if you experience some roller-coaster emotions. You may feel excited and terrified, ecstatic and miserable, overjoyed and overwhelmed—all at the same time! When the campus looms into view, you may even wonder, "Did I make an awful, dreadful, terrible mistake?"

No, you didn't, unless you asked God to stay at home! He's been with you from the start, so He won't desert you now! Trust Him to guide you into what's best as you seek His personal direction for you each day. Read His Word. Talk to Him. Then listen.

This book will help. Early in the morning, late at night, or in the hours between, use these pages in your regularly scheduled time of devotions. At the end of each day's reading, you will find a prayer to get you started in your talks with God. Tell Him what you're thinking, feeling, or wondering. Talk to Him about every high point and low spot you experience. Give Him your praise and your concerns.

You will also find space in these pages for you to journal. To do that, just write down whatever comes to your mind during your devotional time. This will help you to stay close to the Lord. And journaling will help you take note of your first days in college—the college where you've been accepted! The place where you've been directed by God.

PRAYER: Heavenly Father, thank You for guiding me to the college that's right for me. I don't know what to expect, but I'm glad You do. Help me to stay near You, Lord. Thank You for being with me always. In Jesus' name.

JOURNALING WITH GOD: Talk with God about how well He knows you and how well you know Him.

_____

_____

God sets the lonely in families.

(Ps. 68:6, NIV)

Freshmen usually come a few days early for orientation, so when you arrive, you may see a lot of bewildered-looking people on campus. To be truthful, you probably look the same to them! But don't let that throw you. Just concentrate on what comes first—finding your dorm!

As soon as you locate your dormitory room and stow your belongings, you will have a reference point for your personal orientation. Then everything on the campus will be oriented toward where you left your CD player or portable fridge!

Most likely, the dormitory to which you've been assigned will not get a five-star rating. Traditionally, freshman get the rooms with broken thermostats, peeling paint, and closets smaller than your luggage. That's to be expected, but the good news is you'll have roomier, less crummy quarters to look forward to your junior and senior years! For now, the freshman dorm is home—or will be.

As you walk through the front door for the first time, the bodies crowding the hall and doorway to your room may make you wonder, "Who are these people? What do they want? Why are they here?" You may even start to ask, "Why am I here?"

You'll remember soon enough. Meanwhile, one of these strange individuals is your new roommate—who is not at all what you expected—so just expect that too! You may not be exactly as envisioned either, but that's okay. That's how it is with families. Relatives relate their similarities and adjust their differences to one another. So welcome your dorm mates who may look altogether different from you, yet bear a striking family resemblance as each of you wonders, "Who are these people? Why am I here?"

PRAYER: Dear Lord, I guess You have a reason for placing me in this place! Help me get to know my dorm family and accept them as the persons You created. In Christ's name.

JOURNALING WITH GOD: What's the first thing you want these people to know about you? Ask God what's important to Him.

_____

_____

_____

_____

_____

_____

And the Lord said to me,
"Mortal man,
pay attention to everything
you see and hear.
I am going to tell you
the rules and regulations
for the Temple."
(Ezek. 44:5, TEV)

"Rules! Rules! Rules!" No one likes them much, but did you ever notice how quickly you used to tell your visiting friends what the house rules were in your family? Say, for example, a friend joined you for dinner and, when everyone sat down, immediately asked you to pass the ketchup. If no one in your family takes the first bite until someone says a blessing, you might have answered, "Sure, just as soon as we say grace." Maybe you didn't want the person to offend your parents. Maybe you wanted to avoid an awkward scene. But, most likely, you wanted your friend to feel comfortable—to feel right at home.

Knowing house rules is an important part of feeling at home in your new surroundings. Just as you let your friends know what to expect in your house, your college home advisors will let you know what to expect too.

Each college or university has a student handbook, and some will have your copy waiting for you in your room. It's a "rule book," but its contents let you know what's okay and what isn't. On your desk, you may find a list of dormitory regulations. If not, it may be posted on the back of your door and on a bulletin board in the hall. Also, the RA (Resident

Advisor or Resident Assistant) on your floor (or somewhere nearby) will help you know the house rules. That person may even be waiting to greet you when you arrive. So pay attention to what you see and hear. God will use these helps to teach you the rules and regulations of His Temple—which is any place you happen to be!

PRAYER: Heavenly Father, thank You for making Your home in and with me. Help me to feel at home quickly in this place. In Jesus' name.

JOURNALING WITH GOD: In what ways do you feel at home with God?

_____

_____

_____

_____

_____

_____

_____

_____

Therefore say,
Thus saith the Lord God:
"I will even gather you
from the people,
and assemble you
out of the countries
where ye have been scattered,
and I will give you the land."
(Ezek. 11:17, KJV)

Orientation involves "assembling the people." As your freshman class comes together for the first time, you'll notice people from almost every racial and ethnic background milling around the campus. If your college has a cultural exchange program, you'll see an especially brilliant display of color and dress as individuals bring whatever is familiar to them to this new place.

In the next few months, you'll get to know some of these people and their faces well. Many of them will soon recognize you. But as you initially come together on unfamiliar ground, remember: you're not alone. God is with you, of course. And every new freshman is with you too.

Few of you have met, yet you have much in common. Each of you feels somewhat disoriented, or the school wouldn't be having freshmen orientation! Each of you has varying degrees of doubts. Each of you has recently left behind the family, home, friends, and cultural environment that you know best.

So look at the variety of people gathered from this and other countries, and see the communal bond. No matter how unusual a person may seem to you, everyone who has assembled for orientation has something special in common. Each of you will now receive the land! That's right—the land. For some freshmen, "receiving the land" means coming to a new country, new state, or new environment to acquire an education. For others, this means the proverbial land of opportunity. For still others, this means anything from landing a better job in the future to having a good time without landing in trouble! But when you think about it, "receiving the land" means all of that to all of you!

Is it possible, then, that these strangers are not really foreigners after all? Sure, you feel like aliens! But as each of you gathers in this new place, you come to common ground. Differences drop away as you receive a common gift: the land, the campus, the community of peoples and opportunities which God has given you.

PRAYER: Dear Lord, thank You for Your good gift in bringing me to this campus. Help me to receive what You've given and accept other people graciously. In Jesus' name.

JOURNALING WITH GOD: Ask God to show you anything in you that's foreign to Him.

DAY 5

For the Lord's sake
accept the authority
of every human institution.
(1 Pet. 2:13, NRSV)

During Orientation Week you'll hear plenty about campus rules. However, your college isn't the only institution with regulations you're expected to accept without question! You will find that other organizations have expectations too.

In the auditorium, gym, or some other place of assembly on Orientation Day, you may see booths with displays telling about campus activities and clubs—all of which have membership rules, regulations, or requirements. You may also see booths set up by banking institutions.

Sometimes local banks work with a college by offering student checking accounts. These usually come with no service charge or a minimal fee of, say, one dollar per month that most students can afford. The idea is to provide you with a safe place to stash your cash while giving you a means of writing checks for tuition, lab fees, books, or other needed supplies. (This may or may not include concert tickets, tapes, and T-shirts from your favorite music group!)

The institutions in or near your campus have your well-being in mind. They're here to help. In return, they expect you to submit to requirements or regulations they established long ago. Those rules have the institution's best interests—

and yours—at heart. But, in essence, they all have the same bottom line: *Don't withdraw too much! And try not to cause any trouble!*

Can you live with that? Of course you can! Even if the rules seem nitpicking, you can remind yourself that they must have been made for some reason. You can also be assured that God instituted these institutions!

They may think they're in business to make money, but you know better! They're around because God allows them to be. They exist to serve, protect, and help you. Now, all you have to do is whatever they say!

If that seems tedious, just remember, it's God and His authority to whom you're really submitting. For your sake, He provides institutions. For His sake—and the good of the name "Christian"—it's up to you to obey.

PRAYER: Dear Lord, I don't want to do anything that reflects badly on the name of Christ. Help me to obey You by being cooperative with those You have placed in authority over me. Bless this institution and other organizations around this campus with Your leaders, Your spirit, and Your purpose. In Jesus' name.

JOURNALING WITH GOD: Ask God to show you any resistance you have to authority. Ask Him to show you areas in which you're inclined to withdraw.

11

*To every thing
there is a season,
and a time to every purpose
under the heaven.*
(Eccl. 3:1, KJV)

If you've chosen a small college or university, you may have already registered for classes. Some schools encourage new students to set a telephone appointment with a counselor to discuss needed courses and arrange a workable schedule. With the right computer software, a school can even allow new students to go ahead and register by phone. So maybe you've registered for your individual classes and just need to find out where they're located. If so, you need a map of the campus. If not, you need to make some sense out of that thick catalog you've been pouring over for months!

As you become oriented to college catalogs and campus life, you'll discover counselors and student advisors nearby to help. They can clarify areas of confusion. They can let you know which subjects are required of all students. They can advise you about specific courses in the general subject area in which you plan to major.

If you don't yet know what your major area of study will be, don't worry. You have plenty of time to decide. Right now, however, you need to select courses for this semester and then act on those choices. You pick the subject. You find the appropriate class. You schedule your time.

Keeping in mind that there are X number of class hours you need to take, X hours in which to study, X in which to sleep, eat, or do anything else that needs doing, you can plan your time accordingly. The catch is, you've never done this before, so you have no way of knowing if your schedule—which looks great on paper—will even work!

Again, this is where advisors help. For instance, your counselor may say, "I think you're taking on too much. How about giving yourself a little more free time this first semester while you adjust to college life?" Your advisor may suggest an alternate course that's less strenuous than what you had in mind. Or maybe you've chosen a semester of weaving baskets (inadvertently, of course), and your counselor will point that out.

Regardless, your schedule is your decision. It's not set in cement, but it is set into motion! It can be set in season too. How? As you seek God's purpose and timing for your first days in college, trust Him to advise your advisors and counsel those who counsel you.

PRAYER: Heavenly Father, You alone know the unknown. Only You have set the seasons and scheduled the night and day. Thank You for caring how I spend time. Thank You for leading me toward Your purpose for me. In Jesus' name.

JOURNALING WITH GOD: Ask God to show you His plan for your time. Ask Him how His timeliness and timelessness affect you.

Observe the Sabbath
and keep it holy.
You have six days
in which to do your work,
but the seventh day
is a day of rest dedicated to me.
(Ex. 20:8–10, TEV)

By the time Orientation Week comes to an end, you should have a pretty good idea of where everything is located in relation to your dorm. By now, you've found the bookstore, auditorium, cafeteria, and any other place you can't live without. So you've surely found the campus chapel too!

As you become more oriented to college life, you may feel disoriented from the familiar patterns at home. That's inevitable as faces, places, and routines shift to something new. But while everything around you changes, God does not. He remains constant—and so does your constant need for Him.

Already you have chosen a schedule for your time. Next semester, you'll find that changes too! Some of the friends you're making now will drop out before the season ends. The leaves will change color. New teachers will come, and you may alter old views. You may decide to change your schedule; you may change your habits of exercise or sleep or food. You may stop writing friends at home. But while everything around you changes, God does not. He remains constant—and so does your constant need for Him.

Finding a new church home on campus or in the community nearby may not be comfortable at first. But worshiping

God with other people who come to worship Him will be comforting. At this point of new beginnings, you no longer have parents or other caretakers urging you, "Come on! Get up! It's time to get ready for church." Now, it's up to you to decide how you'll begin your first days in college.

Will you take a risk from the start and make it clear to dormmates that you're a Christian? Will you allow worship time as you schedule your work, studies, or other activities? Will you dedicate a needed day of rest to God?

New routines do not just happen. They're arranged. It is totally up to you to decide. But while everything around you changes, your basic needs do not. Remain constant in God, knowing His constant need for you.

PRAYER: Heavenly Father, I love and adore You! I praise You for Your power and majesty and might—even if I don't always understand what that means! I do know I need You, Lord. I even need You to draw me into worship! Help me to set apart constant, regular, faithful time for You and other Christians. In Christ's name.

JOURNALING WITH GOD: Write down all the ways that you adore God.

_____

_____

_____

_____

_____

DAY 8

I will instruct you
and teach you
in the way you should go;
I will counsel you
and watch over you.
(Ps. 32:8, NIV)

As your classes begin, you'll probably feel a mixture of nervousness and excitement—nervous as you wonder what's expected of you; excited as you enter a challenging level of study. If some of your semester hours involve required subjects that don't really hold your interest, you might also find yourself feeling scared, worried, or just plain annoyed!

"Why do I have to study this?" is a question most new students ask, and maybe you will too. But don't necessarily expect to find a logical or satisfying answer! Instead, ask yourself the real question: Am I teachable? Am I willing to learn?

It's not that your feelings, interests, and abilities do not matter. They most certainly do! How you feel, what you enjoy, and where you're capable are the very aspects of yourself that will help you to know what major area of study you're eventually to pursue.

In the meantime, you need to know that some subjects do not appeal to you because no one made them appealing! Even a lively subject can be presented in such a ho-hum fashion that people who are naturally gifted in that area have to labor to listen or strain to stay awake!

College studies may not be different. But just maybe they will. Choose to find out. Allow your new instructors ample time to entice you with interesting material that you've never before considered. Listen. Learn. Give yourself and any unchallenged ability a chance to produce interests that you didn't know you have! And as you get acquainted with your professors, let God instruct you as you listen, learn, and profess His holy name.

PRAYER: Give me a teachable spirit, Lord. Help me to accept Your instructions. In Jesus' name.

JOURNALING WITH GOD: In what ways are you a professor in God?

_____

_____

_____

_____

_____

_____

_____

_____

I am a friend
to all who fear you,
to all who follow
your precepts.
(Ps. 119:63, NIV)

Right when you started to get used to the campus, it's suddenly invaded! With the end of Freshmen Orientation comes a company of upperclassmen who think they're upper class and you're lower than low!

Such attitudes are deeply steeped in tradition. You can wear yourself out in protest if you like, but you won't change them. Your better options include responding good-naturedly when you can and, when you can't, ignoring smarty remarks about freshmen in general.

The best choice, though, is to look for people of all classes—upper, lower, and in between—who bear the name of Christ. Maybe they'll be shy about saying so, but you can usually tell. For instance, you might see a cross around a person's neck or a certain light in their eyes. Maybe you'll hear them talk about their beliefs or use God's name in a respectful tone. Maybe you'll feel an unusually strong kinship with someone you've barely met.

As you begin to recognize faces in your dorm or classes, watch for telling signs that mark other Christians on campus. Single out those persons as the people you will make a point of getting to know. Listen for names to go with faces. Look for kindness in a smile or glance. Feel the warmth or inner recognition you experience in the company of those who keep company with God.

As you look—really look—at the people around you, trust God to give you His discernment. Just ask and He will! And as you look, really look to Him. Then trust Him to make it clear to others that you're His beloved child too.

PRAYER: Heavenly Father, let the words I speak and thoughts I have always be pleasing to You. Help me to be and see the friends. In Jesus' name.

JOURNALING WITH GOD: Talk with God about the kind of friends He wants for you and for Himself.

_____

_____

_____

_____

_____

_____

_____

_____

*But the king answered,
"No, I will pay you for it.
I will not offer
to the Lord my God
sacrifices that have
cost me nothing."*
(2 Sam. 24:24, TEV)

Did you find all the textbooks you need for classes? Did you know they'd be so expensive?

As your parents or financial aid officer can inform you, college funds don't grow on palm trees! Even second hand textbooks aren't cheap. Neither are lab fees, meal tickets, or other necessities involved in a college education.

You may be fortunate to have scholarship monies to cover these costs. Or perhaps your parents can easily afford them. If not, you may have already begun one of the on-campus jobs reserved for freshmen, such as slinging hash or scraping it off cafeteria plates. If you can type, you may be starting to work in the admission's office where you'll admit name after name after name into a computer bank.

Even if you don't need a campus job, your education will still cost you something. Every day you draw from the non-negotiable but fixed sum of twenty-four hours. Every hour, your class, lab, or study time is at the expense of something else you could be doing.

Maybe you didn't bargain for so much study! Maybe you want a diploma someday but don't really want to spend much time opening books or attending classes. That's your choice. But if you decide to allot too many hours to other activities, your education will probably be short-changed.

As you begin these first days of classes, you also begin establishing new habits. Your routines will either get you by at a reduced rate, or they will get more than your money's worth in obtaining a priceless education. The choice is yours, but so is the cost.

What do you really have to pay for college? The cost of an education is interest. The price of good grades is study. And the big expense is paying attention!

If you have trouble concentrating well on your studies, God can quicken your mind and protect you from distractions. Regularly, daily, and in each moment needed, offer sacrifices of your costly time in seeking Him and His help.

PRAYER: Dear God, I want to do well in school. Thank You for giving me what it takes to be here. Help me to enjoy college life and devote attention to my studies without sacrificing my relationship with You.

JOURNALING WITH GOD: Talk with God about any time-consuming habits He wants you to sacrifice for good.

_____

_____

_____

_____

_____

DAY 11

*When you have eaten
and are satisfied,
praise the Lord your God
for the good land
he has given you.*
(Deut. 8:10, NIV)

So have you praised God yet for the school cafeteria? Hey! Unless the food actually makes you upchuck, it provides you with nutrition, right? Less obvious, however, is the fact that this may be your first college exam!

Food tested the Israelites in the wilderness. Also in the desert, Satan tempted Jesus with food. And long before these wilderness experiences, some very enticing fruit grew in the Garden of Eden!

Remember how the Israelites complained about having manna, day after day? But do you remember why that bread from heaven was called "manna" in the first place? When the people saw it, they exclaimed, "Man hu!" which means, "What *is* it?" or "What's *that?*"

Is this starting to sound familiar? If so, you may be interested in knowing what Moses told the people. "He (God) humbled you by letting you hunger, then by feeding you with manna, with which neither you nor your ancestors were acquainted, in order to make you understand that one does not live by bread alone, but by every word that comes from the mouth of the Lord" (Deut. 8:3, NRSV).

Does that sound familiar too? Aren't those the words Jesus

quoted when Satan tried to get Him to turn a stone into bread? Yes, but what does this have to do with you?

God does not want you to eat stones! He does not want you to break a tooth on biscuits cooked to a hardrock stage! He doesn't want you to gag on greasy fries or wilted lettuce! What God does want is for you to eat the food provided, with thanks given to Him instead of complaints. He wants to see if you will praise Him even if you get stale cake. He wants you to acknowledge His goodness without any bad taste of resentment.

PRAYER: Dear Lord, the food in this cafeteria helps me to understand what it means to give you a sacrifice of praise! But I do choose to praise You for caring about my needs. God, bless those who prepare the meals, those who serve them, and those who eat them. Thank You, Lord, for giving me bread to chew on, spiritually, as I see the value in praying, "God bless this food!"

JOURNALING WITH GOD: Ask God to help you bite into the spiritual truth of feeding on Him by faith with thanksgiving.

_____

_____

_____

_____

_____

_____

*The tempter came
and said to him,
"If you are the Son of God, . . . "*
(Matt. 4:3, NRSV)

Have you noticed how a college campus houses a lot of temptations? There's the temptation of putting your meal ticket into a salad shredder and spending all your money on burgers from a fast-food chain. There's the temptation of staying up all night instead of sleeping, and partying instead of studying. There's the temptation of entertaining thoughts or activities you know your parents wouldn't want you to do! And if you've taken on too much, you may even be tempted to quit altogether.

God understands exactly how you feel. He knows too well the presence of darkness and the power of allurements. He had to allow His own Son to endure temptations of all kinds. First, there was that bit about food. Jesus hadn't had any for forty days! So He was tempted to turn the wilderness rocks into a deli. He was tempted to kill Himself rather than starve to death. He was tempted to use His power for Himself alone rather than the purpose for which it had been given. But do you know what the real temptation was? Jesus felt tempted to prove Himself.

"If you are..." That's the challenge of darkness. *If* you *are* so bright, prove it with 4.0 grades, whether you learn anything or not! *If* you *are* successful, prove it by becoming more so. *If* you *are* "with it," prove it by partying all night with everyone else. *If* you *are* the best athlete, prove it by glomping pills so you can keep playing, despite injuries that could bench you forever. *If* you *are* a Christian, be sappy sweet, wear clothes from the Middle Ages, and let all peoples everywhere use you for a shoe sole scraper.

"If you are..." *If* you *are* what? What do you feel you have to prove? To whom do you think you have to prove it? As you consider these things, remember: being tempted is not a sin. But sin can come by giving in and proving yourself to anyone but God.

PRAYER: Heavenly Father, I need Your help in recognizing the temptations that try to pull me away from You. Help me, Lord, to overcome evil with good and to triumph. In Christ's name.

JOURNALING WITH GOD: Talk with the Lord about every area where you hear yourself saying, "I'm tempted to..."

_____

_____

_____

_____

_____

_____

But Jesus answered,
"The scripture says,
'Man cannot live on bread alone,
but needs every word
that God speaks.'"
(Matt. 4:4, TEV)

Isn't it interesting how almost every culture has a burger equivalent? Instead of a bun, it may have a taco shell, pita bread, or pizza crust. In Hawaii, it may be poi, or in Africa, a bread ball made of cornmeal paste. But the rest of the ingredients are pretty much the same.

However, people can't live on meat, cheese, and tomatoes alone! In the wilderness, the Israelites complained about a lack of onions! But even chopped onion, lettuce, and some kind of bread wrap won't satisfy spiritual hunger.

Inside of every person on earth, there's hunger for a taste of God. The church understands this because Christ Himself understood. He knew that His strength and power came from prayer and from the Word of God. Regularly, He fed Himself on both.

When temptations threatened Him, Jesus did not debate, dispute, discuss, or argue. He did not stay up all night, pleading, conversing, combating, or chatting. He did not haggle, wrangle, quibble, bait, or negotiate. He did not try to reason with the tempter, nor did He try to explain Himself or His position. Instead, He consistently quoted Scripture in the face of evil—as many times as it took!

Satan tried to confuse Him by quoting the Bible right back! But Jesus wasn't fooled. He understood the Word of God too well to twist it into saying something it did not mean. He knew God's will and God's ways by knowing God's Word. And knowing, He overcame.

The good thing about the temptations you face is that they can help you to know yourself better. However, the bad thing about temptations is that you have no power to overcome when you don't know what God has to say.

If you don't know, you can find out! If you don't have a Bible handy, you can get one. Find a reliable translation that speaks to you in a language you understand. Put what you learn into practice by hearing, believing, and living Bible truths. Then overcome your doubts, discouragements, and temptations with God's good Word in you.

PRAYER: Holy Father, I praise You for the comfort, power, and promises of Your Holy Word. Thank You for sending Jesus as Your Word made man.

JOURNALING WITH GOD: Think about the Word of God and what it means to you.

_____

_____

_____

_____

_____

DAY 14

*No testing has overtaken you
    that is not common to everyone.
God is faithful,
    and he will not let you
        be tested beyond your strength,
but with the testing
    he will also provide the way out
so that you may be able to endure it.*
(1 Cor. 10:13, NRSV)

Have you worked out in the gym? If you kept with the program, you may have noticed a nice change in muscle tone after only a few weeks. As you checked out the difference in the mirror, however, your eyes probably skimmed over the absolutely perfect spots and went straight to the ones you still wanted to improve!

God's holiness has already perfected you in some areas. The process may have been so painless that you didn't even say, "Ouch!" You didn't even notice how much you had grown spiritually. But just as you surely notice when you exercise a muscle that's been unused for too long, so will you feel the ouch or stretch of any spiritual area that needs improvement.

Exercise can be a drag, a discipline, a practice session for your favorite sport, or a sport itself. Of course, the dark powers of this world would like to make sport of you! God allows a certain amount of testing from His opponent to provide you with a means of exercising your beliefs. He wants you to keep in shape—to be firm in your faith.

God also wants to help. He gives you confidence and assurance by promising you that He won't allow more than you can bear. That's sort of like spotting you on a balance beam or standing over you to catch the weight if a barbell slips.

The real test, though, is whether you'll exercise the perfect promises in His Holy Word—promises that perfectly fit your spiritual shape and tone. When you claim almost any of God's promises, you'll find a condition about something that's expected of you in return—a condition that helps you get in condition spiritually! So? Just do it!

PRAYER: Dear God, sometimes, temptations are painful and the weight of peer pressure too heavy! I don't want to be the only person on campus going through the way out which You provide! But I choose to do Your will, Lord. I want to be firm in faith and faithful to You. I want to please You more than people! Please give me strength to abide by Your conditions and receive the promises You've given me. In Christ's name.

JOURNALING WITH GOD: Ask God to show you how you're to exercise biblical truths in your life.

_____

_____

_____

_____

_____

_____

DAY 15

*Therefore confess your sins
to one another,
and pray for one another,
so that you may be healed.*
(James 5:16, NRSV)

Now that you've had a couple of weeks in college, have you done anything you regret? Did you fail a test in your dorm by going along with what the crowd was doing even though you knew it wasn't a good idea? Did you treat someone badly? Do you feel ashamed of something you said or did?

As people get used to one another, misdeeds, mistakes, and misunderstandings do occur. That's to be expected when diverse individuals come together for the first time. But that doesn't mean it's OK to keep on hurting yourself or someone else!

Maybe you haven't done that. Maybe you're proclaiming your innocence! But take an honest look at sin. Do you know what it is? The word means to "miss the mark," which makes it rather personal. For example, if you made a promise you didn't keep, you cannot say, "Mark my words!" Your words missed the mark! Or if you feel that God's urging you in one direction and you go another, you've missed the mark in reaching His goal for you.

Often, though, sin includes or affects others because sin involves trespass. This could mean trespassing on holy ground by disobeying God's law. Or it could mean infringing on

30

someone else's privacy, rights, or space by barging in, unwelcomed or uninvited.

As soon as you recognize a problem, you need, of course, to stop the act of trespassing or mark-missing. The next step is to confess—first by admitting the sin to God and praying about the situation. If someone else is involved, you also admit your mistake to that person or others who may have been affected by your actions.

What then? As you ask for God's forgiveness, He heals the mark against you as though it never existed! When He forgives, He forgets, and your relationship with Him is fully restored—or healed.

As you confess your sin to others, your relationship with those persons will at least be heading toward recovery! By going a step further and praying for one another, you invite God into the affected area of the friendship so it too is effectively healed.

PRAYER: Dear God, forgive me for trespassing against You. I don't want to miss Your mark for me. I don't want to hurt other people or myself. Help me to be quick about knowing and admitting the wrongs I've committed. Help me to do Your will in Christ's name and not be at cross-purpose with Him.

JOURNALING WITH GOD: Discuss areas of trespass with God.

_____

_____

_____

*For if you forgive
others their trespasses,
your heavenly Father
will also forgive you;
but if you do not forgive others,
neither will your Father
forgive your trespasses.*
(Matt. 6:14–15, NRSV)

Someone swiped your only clean towel and returned it wet! Someone read a letter from the person you dated in high school! Someone ate your last chocolate chip cookie from home! Then when you couldn't sleep for thinking about these things, someone next door kept turning up the volume on a late-night TV talk show that you don't even like!

No doubt about it, these people have trespassed against you! Now what are you going to do about each situation? If you insist on having your towel cleaned, you may never see it again. If you get your cookie back, you wouldn't exactly want it. No one can unread your letter, and the TV talk finally stopped chattering. So what do you do? Nothing? Wrong!

You set limits on yourself, don't you? Well, you may need to set them on other people too. They may not know they have trespassed against you if you don't tell them. They may keep on if you don't say anything. By remaining silent, you can actually encourage behavior that could easily stop.

You don't have to have a major confrontation though. Usually, it's enough to say, "If you want something of mine, just ask! But *do* ask." Depending on your personality, you can use brevity or wit. You can also make a choice to use a kind voice!

But what if nothing you say does any good? What do you do then? Find a way to hide your valuables and lock up your stuff! Buy ear plugs if you have to! But before the day ends, make a deliberate decision to forgive.

PRAYER: Heavenly Father, I'm not used to people coming into my room at odd hours or borrowing my things without asking. I don't much like noise when I'm trying to sleep! But I like confrontations even less! Please give me the words I need to set boundaries without causing a scene. Help me to forgive, so my trespasses will be forgiven too. Right now, that doesn't sound like much of a bargain! But then, I guess I can't receive Your forgiveness if I'm holding on to anger or resentments. Thank You for forgiving me. Thank You that my forgiving others is not a feeling, but a choice I make. In Christ's name.

JOURNALING WITH GOD: Ask God to remind you of times you have forgotten to forgive; then offer those situations to Him.

_____

_____

_____

_____

_____

*But love your enemies,
do good, and lend,
expecting nothing in return.
Your reward will be great,
and you will be children
of the Most High;
for he is kind to the
ungrateful and the wicked.*
(Luke 6:35, NRSV)

Your dormmate next door is becoming a pain! You've already gotten tired of loaning your money, clothes, and the use of your CD player. But since you've been asked every time, you've gone along with each request—until now. Now this weird person wants to borrow your underwear! Do you have the right to say no? You certainly do! The catch is: that may not be what God wants.

God says to lend to those who ask! That doesn't mean He's not interested in your feelings, property, or rights. He is. But if you belong to Him, then everything you are and everything you own belongs to Him too!

Look at it this way: From time to time, you change your belongings anyway, right? If you outgrow something or it wears out, you don't care as much about what you had. You probably discard it for something else. Well, feelings have a way of changing too, and so do circumstances. Today's enemy may be discarded by becoming tomorrow's best friend!

Loaning what's asked can be a way of making a friend of someone you've previously disliked. By adding kindness to any request made of you, you've given generously of yourself—as well as your belongings. On campus or off, that's something that only the children of God are apt to do!

Can you see how God can use your kindness to attest to His spirit and love? It make take a while for your dormmates to notice the difference Christ makes in you. But sooner or later, they'll wonder just Who made you the person you are.

PRAYER: Dear God, I'm beginning to see why everyone doesn't choose Your narrow way! It's so narrow, I can't get through unless I'm willing to drop everything I'm carrying! I can't always say I like it, but if I'm going to be known as Your child, I want to take after You! Help me to be as generous as needed to bring You honor. And thank You, Lord, for Your perfect reward. By emptying my hands and pockets, I have more space for receiving Your Holy Spirit. In Christ's name.

JOURNALING WITH GOD: Listen as God reveals to you His view of ownership.

_____

_____

_____

_____

_____

_____

DAY 18

*Thou shalt love thy neighbor
as thyself.*
(Lev. 19:18 and Matt. 19:19, KJV)

Great news! Nowhere in the Bible does it say, "Thou shalt *like* thy neighbors!" You just have to love them!

Sometimes, loving people is easy. Sometimes, it's not—especially when you're in close quarters like a dorm! But you'll find you *can* love anyone if you understand what love really means.

First Corinthians 13 provides a handy checklist for you to refer to: Love is patient, kind, and hopeful of eventually seeing the best come through in a person. Love is not pushy, cranky, cocky, resentful, or rude. Love loves truth and does not like to see anything terrible happen—even to truly terrible people! Love wishes people well and always works for their well-being.

With such love in mind, you still may need to get new neighbors! It's not that you no longer care about the ones you have. Regardless of what they do, you can love them and want only their good. Sometimes, though, you need to do that from the safety of another room!

If you find yourself constantly treated with rudeness, unkindness, and resentments—no matter what you do—it may be time to remove yourself from that person's company.

If your roommate goes so far as to threaten you—verbally, physically, emotionally, or spiritually—you definitely do not need to stay in that situation.

"But what about turning the other cheek?" you may ask. Good question! Taken in context, that command of Jesus concerned threats from those in political authority. Today, that would be the equivalent of, say, having an FBI agent hit you—in which case, you would probably be better off if you did turn the other cheek until everything got straightened out! But you wouldn't be expected to live with that person!

To share space with a non-Christian who abuses you or brings ungodly choices into your room is not loving! Why? Encouraging crummy behavior doesn't help anybody! Also, you cannot love your neighbor unless you love yourself, and that means caring about your own well-being too.

PRAYER: God, help! I don't want to have such loose limits that everyone feels free to step all over me. But I also don't want boundaries so close that I get my feelings hurt by almost anything people say or do. Help me, Lord, not to be more sensitive to myself and my own needs than I am to those of other people. But help me not to be insensitive to others—or myself. Thank You for Your Word that says where to draw the line. Help me always to be sensitive to Your love and guidance. In Jesus' holy name.

JOURNALING WITH GOD: Ask God to clarify the boundaries needed for the well-being of yourself or someone else.

DAY 19

*For where two or three
come together in my name,
there am I with them.*
(Matt. 18:20, NIV)

One of the greatest blessings you can have at college is a Christian roommate. Lord willing, the two of you may become close friends for life. For now, however, each time you're both at home, Christ Himself is with you. Of course, He won't step out just because your roommate has to go somewhere! But kept in context, the above Scripture indicates that when two Christians are together, power enters the room—your room!

How does this happen? By mutual consent! "I tell you the truth," Jesus said, "whatever you bind on earth will be bound in heaven, and whatever you loose on earth will be loosed in heaven. Again, I tell you that if two of you on earth agree about anything you ask for, it will be done for you by my Father in heaven" (Matt. 18:18–19, NIV).

After saying this, Jesus added, "For where two or three are gathered together in my name, there am I in the midst of them" (Matt. 18:20, KJV). He's not just hanging out, though! As always, the Lord comes to make a difference.

What kind of difference would occur if you and your roommate—or another Christian in your dorm—agreed to pray together? What would happen if you bound any ill will on your floor and loosened the restrictions on Christ's love? Would everything you pray for be done? Well, that depends!

Jesus' love isn't conditional, but like His Father, He may give a conditional promise! This particular passage, for instance, is not a blank check where you can write in anything you want just because another Christian endorsed it too! No, the condition is, "...come together in My name."

You and your prayer partner must agree on what you're to pray for, of course. But since you're asking in His name, Jesus has to agree too! Otherwise, He just may tell you to use your name, not His, and nothing much would happen then.

PRAYER: Heavenly Father, thank You for providing me with Christian friends. I can't think of anything more intimate than praying with another person! It's hard to make the first move, so I'd really appreciate Your helping me with that, Lord. I'd also appreciate knowing exactly what and how You want us to pray. Bring to mind the people or situations You would like for us to offer in prayer, and give us the very words You'd have us pray. In the name, power, and present company of Jesus.

JOURNALING WITH GOD: List any names or concerns that you and a Christian friend agree are in need of prayer.

DAY 20

Bless those who curse you,
pray for those who abuse you.
(Luke 6:28, NRSV)

Someone in your dorm needs prayer. Someone has turned to alcohol or drugs to keep from thinking or feeling so bad. Someone has decided that only sex interests the opposite sex. Someone has lost hope and doesn't want to go on living.

If you know of situations like these, you may need to speak privately to the RA in your dorm. You will definitely want to pray for the persons involved. But—what if people begin to make their problems yours? What if someone swipes your stereo? What if someone steals your notes from an especially difficult class? What if someone robs you of your dignity, courage, or confidence and curses you to your face or behind your back?

Such people would be your enemies. Yet after all these antagonists have done to you, Jesus tells you clearly, "Pray for them." Why? Why would the Lord place such an expectation on you? Doesn't He know how badly you've been treated?

No one knows as well as Jesus about bad treatment! But He not only tells you to pray for your enemies, He prayed for His. One of His last acts on the cross was to pray, "Father, forgive them; for they know not what they do" (Luke 23:34, KJV).

40

The people who treat you badly don't know what they're doing either. For reasons you probably can't imagine, they desperately need help. Therapy might make them able to cope better, or special medication, or maybe even a jail sentence! But nothing will help as much as prayer. Think about it. Surely, no one needs your prayers more than your worst enemies do!

PRAYER: Dear Heavenly Father, praise You for the power of Your forgiveness. I need it now to help me forgive all those who have wronged me in some way. Help those persons to see You in their lives and turn to You with everything that has made them want to hurt other people. Bless them and forgive them, for they don't know what they do. Help them to know and love You. In Jesus' name.

JOURNALING WITH GOD: Ask God to bring to mind the names of people who have wronged you; then pray for each individual.

_____

_____

_____

_____

_____

_____

_____

*For whoever
does the will
of my Father in heaven
is my brother
and sister and mother.*
(Matt. 12:50, NIV)

The first couple of weeks in college have such an unreal quality, they sort of feel like summer camp. You have a lot of adjustments to make to the campus, classes, new faces, and routines. So you may not have had time to notice how homesick you are! By the third or fourth week, however, your schedule and surroundings have become more familiar and less exciting. If you'd wanted sameness, though, you'd just as soon be home!

Some students adapt to homesickness by hurrying back as often as possible. Others sprint to the phone with long distance calls. Some write lengthy letters weekly, or short letters daily, to keep family involved in their lives. Some tape record voice letters onto cassettes and mail them from the campus post office.

Keeping in touch with your family helps you to adjust to college life. It also helps your parents and siblings, who probably miss you a lot more than you realize. If you've been especially close, all of you will experience some degree of grief from the loss of each other's company.

Jesus and His family had such feelings too. His new work

kept Him busy—and sometimes in trouble with religious authorities! His mother and brothers missed Him, worried about Him, and just wanted Him to come home. Since He was most likely the head of the household, His family may also have felt they simply couldn't get along without Him. With those concerns to consider, Jesus may have felt tempted to quit and go home! He may have felt so tired, He just wanted to rest in His own bed. He may have felt so misunderstood by people, He longed for nice, cozy, familiar surroundings. Regardless of how He felt or what His family thought, though, He knew He had to keep on working toward His Heavenly Father's purpose for His life.

So do you! Apparently the Lord has something in mind for you that requires a college education, or you probably wouldn't be here! But just as Jesus understood the quandary of homesickness, so did He recognize its solution. In essence He says, "You won't feel sick for home if you stay well in touch with Me—and with God's family members nearest you."

PRAYER: Heavenly Father, thank You that You are my Father! Thank You for creating me and surrounding me with brothers and sisters in the family name of Jesus.

JOURNALING WITH GOD: Ask God how He would have you keep in touch with your family at home and your family in Christ.

_____

_____

_____

*To one he gave
five talents of money,
to another two talents,
and to another one talent,
each according to his ability.*

(Matt. 25:15, NIV)

As other students and professors get to know you, they may ask, "Do you have any special talents?" You might find that question on an application for a job or for membership in one of the clubs or organizations on campus. Your college advisor or counselor may ask about your abilities too.

The bigger question, though, is—how do you usually respond? Do you shrug your shoulders and say, "I'm not very talented," and then go on to tell about someone in your family who is?

Talent is a funny thing. It has a way of making Christians become embarrassed, evasive, or "modest," instead of pointing toward the Creator of all talent. Talents also have a way of making people feel worthless about what they can do or envious of the abilities of others.

In the Parable of the Talents, Jesus addressed these concerns. Although "talents" in that particular story refers to money rather than giftedness, the results were the same. The multi-talented persons did what was needed to develop those talents for full use. (The wise investment of a good education could have been part of that development!)

But look at the single-talent guy. He only saw that he had less than the others did! To make up for that lack, he didn't feel like working extra hard. Very likely, he told himself, "This talent isn't worth much! I can't do anything with this." So he denied his talent, buried it, and did nothing at all to develop it. Worse, he then complained about the one who gave him the talent in the first place!

PRAYER: Dear God and Creator of all gifts, thank You for the talent You have given me. Forgive me, Lord, for complaining or comparing what I have with what You've given someone else. Forgive me for any hard feelings I've had toward other people in my dorm who seem to have tons of money and talents too! I want to use what You have given me. Help me to concentrate on the studies I need to develop my aptitudes fully. Help me to use talents and money to bring good credit to Your name.

JOURNALING WITH GOD: Ask God to reveal to you any talent you have that you hadn't thought was worth developing. Ask Him what He wants you to do with that gift.

*If a man vow a vow
unto the Lord,
or swear an oath
to bind his soul with a bond;
he shall not break his word,
he shall do according
to all that proceedeth
out of his mouth.*
(Num. 30:2, KJV)

Promises! Promises! For some people, they don't mean much. They'll say almost anything to keep other people off their backs, out of their hair, or under their thumb! When someone later reminds them of what they promised, they'll say something like, "Oh, that's not what I meant!" or "I was just teasing! Why do you take everything so seriously?" They may even deny their words altogether by telling you, "I never said that! You must have misunderstood!"

Pretending or trying to turn the blame onto someone else does not release people from their vows! According to God's Word, a promise is a promise. By making a vow, a person's soul or inner character either binds itself to the truth—or to a lie.

If you've promised God, your family, or yourself that you would go to college, study well, and do everything you could to get a good education, you need to know that saying those words does not make them true! Actions are required to put the words into practice, into motion, and into truth.

Keeping your promise may involve hard work that, at times, can be discouraging. But just as God expects you to honor your vows, so can you expect Him to help by enabling you to do what you said.

The more you become involved in college life and studies the more you can expect obstacles to arise! No matter what tries to stop you from keeping a vow, though, you can expect God to help you remain true to your word—and His.

PRAYER: Dear Father, all of my church life, I've heard about "victorious living," "leaping in faith," or "overcoming in Christ," but frankly they were just a bunch of words! Now I see that's what I need to make it in college! Lord, I need You to help me overcome any obstacle that gets in the way of my education, promise, or goal. I need You to give me the strength to leap over each difficulty with faith. I need the victory of having my most inner self bound to You in word and deeds and truth. In Jesus' name.

JOURNALING WITH GOD: List the promises you've made to other people, yourself, and God. Discuss with Him what concerns you about keeping your word.

_____

_____

_____

_____

_____

_____

*When a man makes a vow
to the Lord
or takes an oath
to obligate himself by a pledge,
he must not break his word
but must do everything he said.*
(Num. 30:2, NIV)

Pledge week! If it's not this week, it will be soon. Then, each fraternity and sorority on campus will screen new students who are interested in joining their activities. But what about you? Is the Greek system to your advantage? As a Christian, should you become involved in something so, well, worldly? Maybe so, maybe not—it depends on what pledge you have to make as a pledge!

In decisions like this, what's right for one person may not be for another. For the most part, however, you can know what's best for you by finding out more about the individual fraternities and sororities represented on campus. What do they stand for and why? What do they require of persons who join them? What are other members like?

Often, a fraternity or sorority attracts people because of its attractive members! One group may have the very best-looking students on campus. Another may have the wealthiest. Still another may include members with the most brains, the most athletic skills, the most popularity, or the most ____ (fill in the blank!). So any group you decide to join will, in some way, reveal your beliefs, your values, and what's important to you.

Before you pledge your support to fraternity brothers or sorority sisters, be sure you won't have to exclude your brothers and sisters in Christ. By keeping your promise in keeping with God's Word, He can then help you do everything you said.

PRAYER: Heavenly Father, I'm not sure if I want to be called by the name of the organization I'm considering, but I know I want to be called by Your name. Help me to have the needed discernment to make a choice that's right for me and pleasing to You. In the blessed name and company of Jesus.

JOURNALING WITH GOD: Talk with God about what's important to you, including any pledge you'd like to make.

_____

_____

_____

_____

_____

_____

_____

_____

*This day I call
heaven and earth
as witnesses against you
that I have set before you
life and death,
blessings and curses.
Now choose life,
so that you and your children
may live.*
(Deut. 30:19, NIV)

Did you know that every day you make life and death decisions? The company you keep, the patterns you set, and the schedule you maintain will either work for or against your own well-being. Those choices may even affect the well-being of other people too!

If you're not sure which club to join or whether or not to pledge yourself to a fraternity or sorority, it may be because it's a life and death decision! Dangerous rites of initiation or hazing have ended on most campuses, but subtle hazards may still exist. For example, a group may require more of your time than you can take from your studies, other activities, or friendships. Should that happen, friendships may die, healthful activity may cease, and grades may lapse into a coma!

It doesn't have to be that way, of course. A fraternity or sorority may be just what you need to feel accepted, to feel as though you belong, to feel at home so you can grow as an individual. Group members can also be a blessing by their life-giving encouragement of you and your goals.

Blessing or affliction? Life-supporting or plug-pulling—

almost any choice has the capacity for both! If you're not sure, ask yourself whether a decision that faces you today will still affect you next week, next year, or in decades yet to come. You don't know what the future brings, but God does! Each choice brings you nearer or further from Him.

PRAYER: Heavenly Father, it really didn't occur to me that my choices may affect my grandchildren! Yet come to think of it, I've heard older people tell how they belonged to this fraternity or that sorority in their college days. It'd be nice to be glad about my decision, years from now. It'd be awful, though, to be embarrassed or sorry! As I decide, Lord, help me to stick by my first choice of life in You. In Jesus' name.

JOURNALING WITH GOD: Get specific with God about His meaning for your individual life in Christ.

*We seemed like grasshoppers
in our own eyes,
and we looked the same
to them.*
(Num. 13:33, NIV)

Just because you're a freshman doesn't mean you're puny! Just because you didn't make the bench on the playing field doesn't mean you're disqualified from sports! Just because the fraternity or sorority you had your heart set on turned you down doesn't mean you're as unacceptable as yesterday's leftover veggie casserole!

If, for some reason, you're feeling like a grasshopper in your own eyes, it's time to blink and look around! Does at least one person on campus know your name? Have you made at least one good grade? Did you find at least one good dish in the cafeteria? Have you figured out how to find your way to at least one class without getting lost?

If you answered yes to at least one question, you may not be hopping around like a little, lost grasshopper after all! Sure, you feel insignificant at first, especially if you're attending college on a very large campus. But you've already made a significant step toward adjusting to your new environment. What? You've already learned at least one new thing, and isn't that why you came to this place—to learn?

After leaving behind the expectations of their Egyptian masters and wandering around the desert for a while, God's people finally saw the place that they'd been promised. But instead of going in and claiming God's good gift, they said something like, "We're too small! We're too new at this! We can't fit in because we're like grasshoppers and that's how other people will see us too!" In fear, they drew back and spent the rest of their lives in the wilderness, claiming barren spots that no one else wanted!

That was not, of course, what God wanted for them. He wanted His people to stop thinking of themselves as insects underfoot and start seeing themselves as the children of the Almighty God! Then other people of other nations just might see Him in them!

PRAYER: God, forgive me for thinking, acting, or even feeling as though I'm a bug to be squashed by any big shot on campus! Help me to see and receive fully the promise of Your Holy Spirit. Help me to look like You to others. In Christ's name.

JOURNALING WITH GOD: Ask God to help you see what He sees when He looks at you.

_____

_____

_____

_____

_____

_____

Have you ever noticed how heads turn when someone who's exceptionally tall or good-looking walks across the campus? That's just human nature. It's not God's nature, though! He created great hair and shapely bodies and brilliant minds to begin with, and He called "good" what He saw. But God is not impressed by popularity, poise, or appearances!

What turns His head is a person's heart. God checks its condition, takes a close look at inner qualities, and sees if He needs to order a stress test or a spiritual EKG! Depending on the person, the EKG may mean He'll check for enthusiasm, kindness, goodness. Or maybe He'll check the person's level of enjoyment, kinship, or gratitude concerning Him. Fortunately, checking other people's hearts is not your job—unless you're called to be a cardiologist or heart surgeon! You may never know what gives people palpitations of fear, pulsating emotions, or a throbbing pain! You can, however, check your own heart toward God, other people, and yourself.

Often, a heart-check involves turning your head toward whatever is bothering you so you can get a better look. Or you may need to check out your attitudes about school, your abilities, or your personal relationships. Maybe you need to look at what you look at! If something or someone frequently distracts you, maybe you should reconsider what you value or how you spend your time.

As you look at your own heart, see if you're too hard on yourself or someone else. See if you've been comparing your appearance, performance, or even your adjustment to school to those of other people. See if you have a heart for God and His Word.

PRAYER: Heavenly Father, thank You for caring so much about me that You take a closer look. Thank You for showing me any dissatisfaction, attitude, or aspect of myself that needs to change. Help me not to compare myself with other people, but only with what You would have me be and do. In Jesus' name.

JOURNALING WITH GOD: Willingly offer your heart to God for examination and ask Him to reveal His heart to you.

_____

_____

_____

_____

_____

_____

Whoever loves money
never has money enough;
whoever loves wealth
is never satisfied
with his income.
This too is meaningless.
(Eccl. 5:10, NIV)

On a college campus, people come from every imaginable background. Some arrive on academic or athletic scholarships, well-equipped to study hard or play hard. Others make it with heavy financial aid and light, unfancy wardrobes. Still others bring along every fashionable outfit, every brand name of shoes, and every imaginable gadget—from Apple computers to zoom lens camcorders. Which students do you think have just money at heart? Any of them, all of them, or none of them do!

Even if a dormmate has too many possessions to fit into the room, material things may not be particularly important to that person. On the other hand it's possible that students who own very little may be continuously dissatisfied with themselves, God, and other people—always comparing, always complaining, always wishing they had more and more and more!

There's nothing wrong with making money, having money, or spending money (within reason, of course!). No, the problem comes from loving money. What happens is that people become less important than the things they own. God becomes less important than what He gives. Lifeless things take on a life of their own, and values get all mixed-up. Instead of loving people and using money, that reverses and becomes something like: Use people. Love money. And forget God—except to be annoyed with Him for not giving at least as much as is given to everyone else!

Remember how God never said you have to *like* people—just *love* them? Well, with money, it's the opposite. He never said you shouldn't *like* or enjoy money. Just don't *love* the stuff, that's all!

PRAYER: Dear God, sometimes I've been dissatisfied with the resources You've given to me, especially when I see what the other students in my dorm have. Forgive me, Lord, for my complaints! Thank You for providing for me. Praise You for being the only Source of love worth having. In Jesus' name.

JOURNALING WITH GOD: Consider what's valuable to you.

_____

_____

_____

_____

_____

_____

No one can serve two masters.
Either he will hate the one
and love the other,
or he will be devoted to the one
and despise the other.
You cannot serve
both God and Money.
(Matt. 6:24, NIV)

As a campus freshman, you don't yet have to declare a major. That's best because as you progress in your studies, you'll learn more about your own interests, aptitudes, and abilities. Also, you'll find out a lot more about career possibilities in various fields. Perhaps you already have a fairly good idea of what you hope to do when you graduate from college. You may go on to advanced studies or opt for additional training of a technical nature. You may decide to start your own business or find employment with another company. Regardless of your present studies or future career, however, you need to decide now to serve God or money.

For Christians, that's not a hard choice to make! Or is it? Be honest with yourself and God. What motivates you to study? What goals do you have in mind? Have you been considering a particular career mainly because you know it pays exceptionally well? That doesn't necessarily mean a big salary. It could be that a job interests you because it's known to have excellent perks and employee benefits, such as lengthy paid vacations and the latest company cars. Or perhaps the work is considered glamorous because of all the money trappings that surround it. As you consider your major area of studies, think about what truly interests you—even if the pay is minimum wage! Think of yourself as the unique individual God created for a distinct purpose, whether that's cheerfully digging trenches or efficiently running a large, international corporation according to biblical standards. Think of your talents as the equipment you need for the work of God through you.

PRAYER: Holy Father, help me to devote my studies, my life, and my work to You. Thank You for Your good gifts and good purpose for me. In Christ's name.

JOURNALING WITH GOD: Assess your interests, experiences, talents, skills, and abilities. Talk with God about His good use for these gifts.

_____

_____

_____

_____

_____

_____

_____

*And why do you worry
about clothes?
See how the lilies
of the field grow.
They do not labor or spin.*
(Matt. 6:28, NIV)

Being outfitted for college can be a big ordeal! You think you have everything you need, and then something new arises—right about the time your parents feel tapped out! Your on-campus job doesn't pay enough for extras, but you can't say yes to a party you'd really like to attend if you don't have anything to wear. You can't go home with your room-mate for the weekend since that short drive takes you to another climate. You can't swim or play tennis or do a number of things without somewhat suitable attire. But even if you have a fantastic wardrobe, there hasn't been enough time to wash the clothes scattered all around your room!

What's a body to do? Seek God and do the laundry! If He can make a sure-to-wilt flower be well-dressed, He'll be even more interested in how appropriately He dresses you! If He can put together an ensemble in the Garden of Eden, He can provide you with decent wearing apparel. Of course, it may already be there beneath your bed, dirty and forgotten!

God knows every need you have—and those you just think you have. He knows how many dirty socks, jeans, and T-shirts you've tossed in the general vicinity of your laundry basket. He knows how far down you've worn the heels on every pair of shoes. He knows the size of your undies and the condition of them too!

More importantly, God knows you! He certainly knows whether or not you need to be in a certain place at a certain time, wearing certain clothes to fit a certain occasion! He may say, "Go ahead." Or He may say, "No, My child. Not this time." He may not always give you a new outfit, but you can always trust Him to provide the perfect fit for you!

PRAYER: Heavenly Father, thank You for knowing what's best for me. Thank You for caring about my well-being in each area of my life—spiritual, physical, emotional, and mental—financial and social too. Forgive me for fretting or worrying about what I'd like to have. Help me to trust You to provide the right things at just the right time for me. Help me always to be well-clothed with Your Holy Spirit. In Christ's name.

JOURNALING WITH GOD: Consider the lily.

_____

_____

_____

_____

_____

_____

_____

DAY 31

Praise be to the God and Father
of our Lord Jesus Christ,
the Father of compassion
and the God of all comfort,
who comforts us in all our troubles,
so that we can comfort those
in any trouble
with the comfort we ourselves
have received from God.
(2 Cor. 1:3–4, NIV).

Congratulations! You've just completed your first full month on campus! So are you ready to go home?

How often you're able to go may depend on how far you are from home and how affordable travel is for your family. If you've come quite a distance on a one-way ticket that all of your relatives emptied penny jars to buy, you may be stuck here a while.

Meanwhile, you know, of course, that you're not alone. You know that God is with you. But if you and a parent or brother and sister have been very close, you'd probably like a hug about now!

Why not let God embrace you with His Word? Try reading a psalm, verses from the Song of Solomon, or a poetic passage from Isaiah. Read some of Paul's encouraging letters to the churches in Galatia, Philippi, or Corinth. Embrace the three little loving letters of John. Or ask God to speak to you personally, then open the pages of your Bible and find a verse that leaps out with comfort or joy.

Let God's Word embrace you emotionally, spiritually, and mentally. Let His promises soothe and console you. Let the power of His Word give you strength.

When you've been strengthened and encouraged, look around. Someone in your dorm lives as far from home as you—maybe farther. So don't keep your consolations to yourself! Give that person the wonderful comfort and compassion that God has given you.

PRAYER: Heavenly Father, I miss my family a lot! I thought I'd be glad to be on my own, and often I am. But right now I just wish I could curl up in my own bed or eat a home-cooked meal. Help me to find Your encouraging word for me this day. Help me to pass on to someone else the comfort found only in You and Your Word. In Jesus' name.

JOURNALING WITH GOD: Find the comfort in each line of the 23rd Psalm.

_____

_____

_____

_____

_____

_____

_____

_____

*I will pour out
my thoughts to you;
I will make my words
known to you.*
(Prov. 1:23, NRSV)

Have you ever seen a film about survival training? The rooky encounters a number of obstacles and must respond well to each. Otherwise, the person will be shot or shoot someone who's innocent! The bullets aren't real, of course, but they make a very real point: Protect yourself from lurking dangers without hurting anyone else.

In a way, your first days in college are similar to a survival training camp. Like other rookies, you can't know what will come up next! You can't possibly guess the exact situations you'll encounter. Yet at each turn, you make choices that could place you or someone else in danger.

Getting shot down by other students or even college professors is one hazard you may face! Plunging into traps set with drugs, alcohol, or sex is another danger. And still another is dropping—with exhaustion or discouragement—so much that you just cannot go on. In dangerous times, the world's protective devices include anything from hand guns to condoms! But that's not The Way to survive. The Way involves protecting yourself by application of God's Word.

What does that really mean? As you read the Bible, make it personal! See how well it fits you and your situation.

Underline passages that speak directly to you. Mark God's promises as your own. Note any conditions attached to those promises, so you'll know what's expected of you. And in the margins of each page, note thoughts that come to you as you read. Then when you feel overwhelmed, you won't be overcome by whatever is troubling you. By merely opening up the pages of your personalized copy of God's Word, you'll easily find the Word that encourages, strengthens, and protects you well.

PRAYER: Holy God, I praise Your loving, comforting, all-knowing power. Thank You for speaking to me in Your Word. Help me to note well and apply Your promises and plans. In Jesus' name.

JOURNALING WITH GOD: Listen to God's thoughts that come into yours as you read His Holy Word. Write down what you hear.

_____

_____

_____

_____

_____

_____

Let the wise also hear
and gain in learning,
and the discerning acquire skill,
to understand a proverb
and a figure,
the words of the wise
and their riddles.
(Prov. 1:5–6, NRSV)

By now you've had a chance to get to know your college professors and form opinions about each class. In some cases, you may grasp everything that's said. In others, you may not have a clue about what's going on! But take heart! You should still have time to correct the situation before mid-terms.

How? The first step is realizing that a problem exists. The next step is identifying it as precisely as you can. Then you can find a workable solution.

For example, the problem may be that you can't quite figure out what one of your professors wants. The solution may be to see where the course is headed by reviewing the syllabus you probably got for that class. If not, review your study notes. Or the solution may be to seek input from another student—preferably one with an understanding of the subject. Or you may need to talk with that professor.

As you try to identify the problem, you may see that you really do understand the material well enough, but the class happens to be at your slump-time. If so, switching to a class that's earlier or later in the day could be the best solution. So could getting more sleep! Or maybe you're in a daily slump from skipping a meal that would give you more energy.

Whatever the problem is, be wise! Do something about it quickly. Gain understanding about your particular situation and personal needs—the sooner, the better. Acquire good skills in caring for yourself so you can be alert and awake in every class. Then you'll be able to hear, understand, and learn.

PRAYER: Dear Lord, You said that if anyone lacks wisdom, just ask, so I'm asking now! Help me to be wise about my use of time—in and out of the classroom. Help me to hear what's said and understand each riddle or quiz. Help me to take care of my studies and myself. In Jesus' name.

JOURNALING WITH GOD: Ask God to give you insight into each problem that you face.

_____

_____

_____

_____

_____

_____

_____

_____

*Everyone who competes
in the games
goes into strict training.
They do it to get a crown
that will not last;
but we do it to get a crown
that will last forever.*
(1 Cor. 9:25, NIV)

During your senior year in high school, did you excel in some way? Were you a star athlete or honors recipient? Did you represent your school in academic competitions, sports, or student government? Were you voted the most popular, best looking, or most likely to succeed? Did you have a prominent role in a club, homecoming, prom night, or the senior class play? Were you class poet or valedictorian?

The higher your achievements during your senior year, the lower you may be feeling now! Instead of the prestige and recognition you received as an upperclassman, you're back at the bottom of the heap! And all of the high school accolades suddenly seem as worthless as an overripe banana!

So what are you going to do about it? For starters, you can remind yourself that the games aren't over yet! This is a new tournament, and you'll probably have other chances for a match of wits or physical skill. Until then, face it! You've been benched! You can water the sidelines with your tears. Or you can take a breather, rest up, and be ready when your turn to play comes again.

Most likely, it will come. But even if it doesn't, you don't have to spend your whole life looking at a tarnished crown or trophy from high school days! Instead, you can compete in another contest—the one between good and evil. In this competition, which includes a stadium that covers the whole earth, you'll have a highly unusual goal: winning over the spectators!

According to game rules, however, you can't win anyone by yourself. You'll need God-given skill and timing, with the Holy Spirit as your coach. You can count on His help, though, simply by choosing to be on Christ's team!

PRAYER: Lord, help me not to feel left-out because there's no spotlight on me now. Help me to enjoy the lessened pressure yet remain flexible and stay in good shape. Keep me mentally, physically, and spiritually alert to Your will and Your perfect timing. In Christ.

JOURNALING WITH GOD: Talk with God about His game plan for people in your dorm who don't really know Him.

_____

_____

_____

_____

_____

_____

*Teach me
    to do your will,
        for you are my God;
may your good Spirit
    lead me on level ground."*
(Ps. 143:10, NIV)

Highs and lows often accompany the first days in college. The exciting highs of arrival quickly plummet into the lows of disappointment when everything isn't as you had hoped. There's the high of making new friends and the low of missing old friends and family. There's the high of a new discovery about your favorite subject and the low of a quiz you weren't ready to take. There's the high of making it on your own and the low of wondering if you'll make it at all!

Up or down, high or low, you can trust the Holy Spirit to lead you onto level terrain. God Himself is unchanging. His will remains a stable, steadying influence in your life. His Word keeps its word.

Whether your emotions, energy, and expectations run high or drop to an all-time low, seek God's constant will for you in each situation. How? By remaining consistent in what you have already been doing!

Your prayer time helps you to release pent-up feelings, but it also releases God's power to work for good. Your Bible reading helps you to check out timeless truths and apply them to the health and well-being of your inner self and the outer life that other people see. Your journaling time helps you to see God's view, so you can keep everything that happens in its proper perspective—His!

Even if your feelings, people, or the conditions around you change from one second to the next, God does not. His truths, love, and forgiveness last forever.

PRAYER: Holy Father, You know how I think and act and feel. If my spirits soar, You're up there with me! If I'm feeling in the pits, You are there. But whether I'm up or down, help me to know Your will for me at the time. Steady me with Your hand. Open my eyes to see You in every situation. Open my ears to hear what You'd have me do. In Jesus' name.

JOURNALING WITH GOD: Has something been making you feel down or elated? Ask God to give you His level view.

_____

_____

_____

_____

_____

_____

_____

*Sometimes there is a way
that seems to be right,
but in the end
it is the way to death.*
(*Prov. 16:25, NRSV*)

Have you ever told yourself, "But everybody else is doing it! There's no reason I can't too!"

Most people have thought that occasionally. The trouble is that following a crowd means "everybody else" is setting your standards for you! Instead of following the Way of Christ that you've deliberately chosen, you go by what's popular at the time (which will soon change) or how you feel at the time (which will also change).

Usually, crowd-following means not following God! His way can be so narrow that people have to take it single-file. You'll seldom see a broad, flattened path to the doorstep of His kingdom. You'll rarely see people clamoring to get inside. But in the opposite direction, you may often see a wide, far-reaching highway that's headed for whatever looks good, feels good, or seems good at the time.

In college, the pavement typically widens to accommodate additional lanes—for drug traffic, sexual transactions, or transportation of alcoholic beverages over the line! Yet if the persons involved had to stop for an inner search about any of those choices, they would probably say, "Hey! What's the problem here? I'm not doing anything wrong."

Now, why would people think that nothing is wrong when a direction clearly points to death? Isn't it because the way seems okay simply because everyone else is doing it? Can't that make a very wrong way seem right?

PRAYER: Dear Heavenly Father, I admit that thinking about right and wrong isn't a popular topic with most people, including me! I don't want to be a stick-in-the-mud, but I also don't want to head in a direction that's unhealthy, unloving, or unwise. I guess that's what a wrong way is—a direction that's hurtful to me, to other people, or to You. Forgive me, Lord, for the times I've fooled myself into thinking it'd be okay to go along with everyone else—even though I felt uneasy. Help me, Lord, to choose Your healing, helpful way. In Jesus' name.

JOURNALING WITH GOD: Stand still before God and consider the direction you're to go in each area that's troubled you.

_____

_____

_____

_____

_____

_____

*A wise child
makes a glad father,
but a foolish child
is a mother's grief.*
(Prov. 10:1, NRSV)

During your first days in college, you'll probably need to ask someone directions to almost anywhere you want to go. Maybe you're trying to find that little pizza place off campus everyone is raving about, or maybe you're looking for the office of one of your professors. But no matter where you're heading, you need signposts to provide some means of telling if you're going the right way.

To head in the right direction spiritually, you can also expect signs. Your peace of mind and an inner sense of knowing what to do can provide clear directional signals. So can the markers gradually set by your parents over the past decade or so.

Unless you happened to be born to someone on the college staff, you won't constantly have your mother, father, or either set of grandparents on campus. But you will have them with you through their counsel or advice. The signposts they have set over the years can still help to reveal the optimum direction for you now.

This assumes, of course, that your family is acquainted with God's ways and has your best interests at heart. If so, you'll need to pray for them—and listen to their advice! If not, you'll need to pray for them, but look for guidelines set by other adults who have become your spiritual caretakers or family in Christ.

Either way, guidance comes to those who hear! You might never have found that pizza place or that professor if you had not first asked for directions. But the next step was to listen carefully to the instructions about the way you should go.

PRAYER: Heavenly Father, thank You for providing signposts to keep me in the right direction. Thank You for Christians who care about me and who love and serve You. Bless my family, including my Christian teachers and church home. Help me to hear and consider what's said. In Jesus' name.

JOURNALING WITH GOD: Talk with God about anything that's been diverting you from what you've been taught.

_____

_____

_____

_____

_____

_____

*In everything,
do to others
what you would have
them do to you,
for this sums up
the Law and the Prophets.*
(Matt. 7:12, NIV)

If you have to travel a freeway to get on or off your campus, you know that large overhead signs mark the entrances, exits, and interchanges with other highways along the way. The type, condition, and numbers of the roads vary as do traffic flow and directional patterns. In some places, you have to exit to the right. In others, you exit to the left. Still other places point you straight ahead. Yet freeways all over this country have something very significant in common: the overhead signs are highly visible so travelers can easily see them.

God has placed a large, highly visible marker over His children too. Instead of standard green, it's a golden rule to follow: "Do unto others as you would have them do unto you." That's the law! God's law. It's also a prophetic word to you about directions.

For instance, if you're unsure how to respond to your roommate, who's going through a hard time, turn things around to see how you'd feel if your situations suddenly were reversed. Would you want your friend to be honest, loving, patient, and understanding of you under similar conditions? Would you want to be told the truth in a kind way, even if it initially hurt to hear the information? Would you want to be given helpful suggestions? A pat on the back? A hug? Or would you rather be left alone until you've had a chance to think things through yourself?

Of course, the big question is whether your roommate wants what you'd want! Maybe so, maybe not. But either way, ask! Like traffic flow on a freeway, the Golden Rule allows for various entrances and exits to keep ongoing relationships in line and moving smoothly ahead.

PRAYER: Dear God, it's hard enough to treat other people the way I'd like to be treated. If I have to treat them as they want to be treated, I'll really have a hard time keeping up! So Lord, I need You to help me to be there for my roommate without getting in Your way. In Jesus' name.

JOURNALING WITH GOD: Ask God to give you His insight into your roommate's wants and needs.

_____

_____

_____

_____

_____

_____

_____

_____

DAY 39

First take the log
out of your own eye,
and then you will see clearly
to take the speck
out of your neighbor's eye.
(Matt. 7:5, NRSV)

Is your roommate or someone else in your dorm bugging you? No matter what you say or do, that person tells you, "Never mind! You just don't get it!"

Being together has become about as much fun as having a clump of eyelashes stuck in your eye! You've tried to be patient. You've tried to be understanding. You've tried to be a good listener. Now what?

Stop trying! Instead of working so hard to maintain this friendship, you may need to back off and get that chunk of lashes out of your eye. You could brace yourself to gouge around blindly, if you like. But you'll have better results if you simply turn on a light and take a real close look in the mirror. What do you see? Can you find any resentments there? Can you see if you've been stuck in unforgiveness or hurt feelings toward this person? Have you discovered that you've been keeping track of every little thing your friend has done that you didn't like? Have you kept a log in your eye? As soon as you recognize any record-keeping you've done of other people's wrongs, you can by all accounts remove it! Confess the log, give it to God, and receive His forgiveness. But just as if you'd removed those eyelashes, you'll also receive something else. You'll get your sight back! Then—and only then—can you see clearly enough to help with whatever is troubling your friend.

PRAYER: Dear Father, I knew my friend had a problem, but I didn't know I did too! Forgive me, Lord, for blinking back my own feelings. I don't want to keep a record of resentments or hurts of any kind. Help me to let go and turn them over to You. Help me to see clearly Your loving restoration. In Christ's name.

JOURNALING WITH GOD: Ask God to turn on His light so you can clearly see the real issues affecting your dorm-mate and you.

_____

_____

_____

_____

_____

_____

_____

_____

_____

If another member of the church
sins against you,
go and point out the fault
when the two of you are alone.
(Matt. 18:15, NRSV)

Do you know what happens when two friends get together to discuss a third friend? Three people may wind up going three separate ways!

If you've been having a problem with another Christian in your dorm, talk about the situation in private with the person who's involved. With a kind tone and words, tell them exactly how you feel. State your view factually, without letting in any innuendos, accusations, or emotionalism. Just stick to the facts as you see them and avoid dredging up anything from the past, unless it has direct bearing on the situation now.

When you've said what you have to say—as briefly as possible—give the person the courtesy of listening. Even if you would have handled things differently, generously give the benefit of the doubt. It may be that your words or actions contributed to a misunderstanding. If so, be quick to admit your part in the matter. Ask forgiveness, but give it too! Then pray with your friend in Christ, asking God to restore your relationship.

If the person refuses to listen, just try again later! This time, though, you'll need to bring along another Christian friend. That can be risky since there's always a possibility that you're in the wrong, and they'll both say so! However, the idea is not to choose up sides. It's to follow biblical instruction in dealing with a trespass against you. It's to help a wrong be righted so that hopefully it won't happen again!

PRAYER: Lord, I didn't realize that dorm housing has room for so many confrontations! Even the Christians I've met come from different denominations and upbringings, so none of us has exactly the same view. I guess we would, though, if each of us only had Your viewpoint. Help us to see. In Jesus' name.

JOURNALING WITH GOD: Ask God to give you His view of what's happening between you and another Christian.

Let us behave decently,
as in the daytime,
not in orgies and drunkenness,
not in sexual immorality
and debauchery,
not in dissension
and jealousy.
(*Rom.* 13:13, NIV)

All right! Party time! You've been working hard, studying hard, and making some hard adjustments. Now it's time to play!

One friend wants you to come to a frat party. Another wants you to go to an away ball game. Another wants you to go on a picnic. You've also been hearing about a concert in town. So—which do you choose?

Where you spend your leisure hours depends on a number of factors, such as your interests, your available time, the people who will be involved, and your general expectations. You can't know for sure what to expect or what will happen in any given place at any given time, of course, but you will probably have some fairly strong suspicions!

Listen to your concerns. But before you rule out any one possibility, consider the options for each event. Think about the uncomfortable situations which could easily arise and what, if anything, you could do about them. For instance, if things got out of hand at a party, would you be willing to leave? Could you find a quick exit? Could you get back to your dorm without any difficulty?

What about the ball game, picnic, or concert? Would you be stranded in an out-of-the way spot on unfamiliar terrain? Would someone else be with you who has similar concerns about the crowd, the occasion, the atmosphere?

Will the picnic be too intimate? Will the ball game be with your school's arch rival, where mob scenes and fights traditionally erupt? Will the concert be a bash—literally—as guitars, eardrums, and people get smashed?

Wherever you plan to go, find the nearest exit! Invite Christian friends. Then, have a great time—as long as the Light of Christ remains around you. If darkness sets in, you can be sure it's time to leave!

PRAYER: Heavenly Father, a party can turn out to be tame, and an innocent-sounding picnic or away-game can host trouble! I have no way of knowing exactly what will happen, but You do. Thank You for leading me into good times—not bad! Thank You for creating laughter and fun and joy. In Jesus' name.

JOURNALING WITH GOD: Ask God to help you discern the kind of activities that daylight reveals and those that prefer places to hide.

_____

_____

_____

_____

_____

Everything is permissible—
but not everything is beneficial.
Everything is permissible—
but not everything
is constructive.
(1 Cor. 10:23, *NIV*)

One of the advantages of living on a college campus is that you no longer have to ask your parents for permission to come and go. That's also one of the disadvantages!

Once parental supervision lifts, some students aren't interested in going out, but going wild! If their comings and goings have been heavily monitored in the past, they may want to race full speed toward former restrictions. As far as they're concerned, anything and everything goes!

Whether this is true for you depends on you! Your parents aren't around to say yes or no to anything you want to do, on or around the campus. They can't easily impose their standards on you. But standards will still exist. The difference is that you'll set them yourself. So? What will you now give yourself permission to do? What's permissible for you? The answer is anything that you decide to allow! But the catch is that whatever you allow has to be okay with you. Otherwise, you really haven't given yourself permission.

Have you? Will the standards you set be okay for your physical, mental, and spiritual health or safety? Will your choices be okay for your emotional and social well-being? Will your permission be beneficial to you, or detrimental?

Will your decisions be constructive in your relationships with God and other people, or will the outcome be inclined toward destruction of values, property, and persons? What is really, really okay with you?

PRAYER: Dear Father God, are You trying to show me that rules aren't meant to be a line to step over but to step by? One of Your first acts in creation was to separate darkness from the light. Help me to walk lightly and remain in step with You. In Jesus' name.

JOURNALING WITH GOD: Discuss with God anything you'd like to allow yourself.

_____

_____

_____

_____

_____

_____

_____

_____

*Everything is permissible for me—
but not everything is beneficial.
Everything is permissible for me—
but I will not be mastered
by anything.*
(1 Cor. 6:12, NIV)

Have you mastered any of your subjects yet? Have you mastered your favorite sport? Hopefully, you have already mastered the natural inclination most college students have of staying up too late to stay awake in class!

Mastering something puts you in charge instead of the other way around! For instance, when you were little, you mastered riding a bike, jumping rope, or skating. In grade school, you mastered addition, subtraction, and use of the alphabet. In high school, you learned to master a steering wheel, traffic, and car bumpers. Then, having mastered them, you had less tickets, better report cards, and fewer scraped knees or fenders!

You probably don't yet have a complete grasp of all your college material. You may not have a completely restful sleep pattern worked out just yet. Maybe you don't yet control a ball the way you'd like in baseball, basketball, football, tennis, hockey, or soccer. But has anything mastered you?

Each day, you make decisions about what you'll permit yourself to do, say, or even think. Some decisions are big; some aren't. Some affect you greatly; some hardly affect you at all. But before you make any decision, ask yourself if that choice will let something or someone other than God be in control of you. God wants you to serve Him, but He does not want you to be enslaved! No manipulative person or addiction, no obsession or possession has God's permission to master you. Any permission given is what you decide to grant.

PRAYER: Dear God, thank You for giving me the freedom to choose. Thank You for a country and a college where so many good choices are possible for me and my future. Help me not to be mastered by evil, but to overcome everything with good. In the name of the one Lord who is God and Father of all.

JOURNALING WITH GOD: Talk with God about His lordship.

_____

_____

_____

_____

_____

_____

_____

DAY 44

So whether you eat
or drink
or whatever you do,
do it all for the glory of God.
(1 Cor. 10:31, NIV)

"Jesus drank wine, right? So what's wrong with having a glass of it now and then or maybe a beer or two? It's not like I'm getting smashed or drinking hard stuff."

If you've ever had those thoughts, you may need to know that there's no such thing as soft alcohol! The percentage of alcohol in wine or beer averages to the same alcoholic content that you'll find in a mixed drink. You also need to know that in Jesus' day, water was often scarce and already polluted! Also, there weren't waste water management plants, so wine provided a beverage that was relatively free of germs and bacteria. When added to water, the alcohol in the wine acted as a purifier, making the water safer to drink.

A few decades later, the Apostle Paul told his young friend, Timothy, that a little wine might help his stomach. Paul could have gone on to say that too much wine could eat a hole in it! But a small amount apparently helped Tim with a digestive problem, and a seltzer might do the same for you.

Whether you drink wine, swizzle seltzers, or eat the feet of a caterpillar, can you eat and drink for the glory of God? If revulsion at the sight of certain foods makes you turn your head or aversion to alcohol turns your stomach, you won't glorify God by eating or drinking! Nor is He glorified when His children pig out on food or lap up booze.

To put such decisions into perspective, look at the key: "glory." In Greek, it's *doxa*—the same root word found in doxology. Doxa refers to one's honor or reputation. So what you eat and what you drink contributes to your reputation— or lack of it! But because you're a Christian, your eating and drinking habits also reflect on the honor, reputation, name, and glory of God.

PRAYER: Dear Lord, sometimes I forget my health and well-being, and I don't think about how my reputation reflects on Yours. Help me to be considerate of You and the life You've given me. In Jesus' name.

JOURNALING WITH GOD: Talk with God about your reputation on campus—and His.

*Do not get drunk on wine,
which leads to debauchery.
Instead, be filled with the Spirit.*
(Eph. 5:18, NIV)

Even if you haven't felt too close to God lately, you're fairly sure He doesn't want you to get drunk! You can pretty much guess He'd be grieved to see you controlled by alcoholic spirits and given to disorderly conduct or a DUI so you can figure that He'd rather you abstain altogether or stay away from anything that might have control over you—even if it's only for a night.

When you really think about it, you're positive that a loving God wouldn't want anyone He created to be wasted. He couldn't possibly wish a hangover on anyone! Yet since such things do occur, you realize that you'd rather not spend most of the night hanging over a toilet or most of the next day nursing a horrendous headache.

Nevertheless, the choice is yours, and you have the power to fill yourself with anything you want, right? But do you realize you can be filled with something more potent than alcohol and more mood-elevating or mind-altering than drugs? According to God's Word, you can *choose* to be filled with the Holy Spirit. How? Just ask, and you'll receive! Just receive, and you'll be filled!

If you've been feeling down, don't even think about getting

high on needles, pills, or bottles! Don't even once consider soaking your sorrows in alcohol or masking moods and disappointments with drugs. Instead, be filled with the joy, excitement, and power of God's own Spirit! Things can't help but be lighter then.

PRAYER: Dear God, sometimes I feel so down, it's scary! Yet I know You said that whatever Your children ask in Christ's name will be given, so I'm asking now. I need You, Lord! I want Your Holy Spirit to fill and heal and guide me always. In Jesus' name.

JOURNALING WITH GOD: Ask God to show you the difference His Holy Spirit makes in you.

DAY 46

*The body is not meant
for sexual immorality,
but for the Lord,
and the Lord for the body.*
(1 Cor. 6:13, NIV)

If you're living in a coed dorm, you may have seen more body parts than you intended! En route to separate showering facilities, robes fly open, and towels have a way of dropping off in the hall. The close proximity to family life may make you feel like you accidentally caught a glimpse of a brother or sister. But you may find you're interested in taking a longer look.

Curiosity about the opposite sex is natural. From the first little talk about "the birds and the bees" to the heavy breathing in TV soaps or movies, sex appeal has appeal! But even a tastefully-done sex education class may leave people in the dark! So how about some light on the subject?

God created sex and called it good for a good reason: He made people, male and female, for a unique bond that provides special closeness and creates other human beings. As you know, sex education and sexual precautions usually concern the latter—i.e., the creativity part and how to avoid it. What's often overlooked, however, is the agony of having that special closeness between people who just met! Yet a sexual encounter creates a strong and very real bond between those two people—not just physically, but emotionally and spiritually too. As one body joins another, both take on an emotional commitment and also the spiritual commitment of the other person. So while concerns about AIDS and poorly timed pregnancies are certainly very important factors in a sexual encounter, another question must be asked: To whom and with what do you want your emotions—and the Lord's own Spirit—to bond?

PRAYER: Heavenly Father, when Your Word talks about being united in Christ, I understood this as a spiritual and even emotional bond, but I hadn't thought about it as a physical reality too. Yet as Your Spirit fills me, my body houses Your Holy Spirit, so we must be physically united. We're one! Thank You, Lord, for joining Yourself with me in body, mind, and spirit. Thank You for protecting me from any other union apart from You. Help me to be faithful to You always. And Lord, if I'm to marry someday, I pray that You will provide the perfect partner for me—mentally, physically, and spiritually. In Christ's name.

JOURNALING WITH GOD: Ask God about the specific individual or type of person who is right for you.

If we confess our sins,
he who is faithful and just
will forgive us our sins
and cleanse us
from all unrighteousness.
(1 John 1:9, NRSV)

What happens if you've already encountered sexual or other experiences that weren't healthy for you? What happens if you've sinned against God, another person, or your own body? Do you now have to be miserable forever? No! You can't undo the past, of course, nor the consequences of your mistakes. Every action sets a reaction into motion that only time can still. Meanwhile, will you be forgiven?

Forgiveness from God is your choice! Why? God hasn't allowed Himself an option in the matter. He has already given His Word that He will forgive sins confessed to Him, and so that's what you can count on Him to do! He cannot go back on His Word or withhold what He's promised—*if you agree* to the conditions that He pre-set. God's forgiveness does have certain conditions. He says He will forgive you *if you agree* to forgive others. He says He'll forgive you *if you agree* to give what needs forgiving to Him. In other words, you have to give for Him to for-give. Simple, huh? Unfortunately, it's not always easy!

The difficulty in giving sin to God is that you first have to see it and recognize it for what it is. Then you have to admit it's there. If, for example, you're in denial and will not confess

to any wrong-doing on your part, then that particular sin—
and its ill effect—doesn't go anywhere! It remains in you,
continuing to cause you trouble, grief, anger, shame, or some
other upsetting emotions.

The good news, though, is that no sin is too large or too
small for God to handle. Through the perfect life, death, and
resurrection of His Son, He cleanses whatever isn't right—
and that makes you right with Him!

PRAYER: Dear Holy Father, You know what I've done.
Thank You for encouraging me to know too and to bring this
sin to You for Your forgiveness and redemption. I offer it to
You in the name of Your Son, Jesus Christ, who has Your
power and authority to make all things right again.

JOURNALING WITH GOD: Ask God to show you anything
you haven't admitted into His forgiveness.

_____

_____

_____

_____

_____

_____

_____

DAY 48

*If, however, the watchman sees
the enemy coming
and does not sound the alarm,
the enemy will come
and kill those sinners,
but I will hold the watchman
responsible for their death.*
(Ezek. 33:6, TEV)

College dorms don't offer much privacy! Every now and then, though, you'll be alone for a while. During those times, you may find yourself reflecting on past mistakes or things you wished you hadn't done. If so, maybe you realized how hard it is to get into sin all by yourself!

Sinful solos are possible, but sins more commonly involve more than one person! For instance, lying, cheating, and stealing imply the presence of another person who's lied to, cheated, or robbed. Drunken brawls, orgies, and pot parties invite others to participate. And sexual misconducts involve mixing or matching body parts with someone else! But here's the rub: As you become aware of the dangers of a sin, it's up to you to make anyone else who's involved become aware of those dangers too.

Ever since time and hearts began to tick, people have asked, "Am I my sister's conscience? Am I my brother's keeper?" According to God's Word, you are! Oh, you're not meant to be anyone's savior. Only the Lord Jesus Christ can heal, save, redeem, and restore. But you are warned to warn others if you see that something bad is about to happen.

If you don't give a warning, you're accountable. You'll be held responsible for the ills that befall the other people who didn't see trouble coming. If, however, you do speak up but no one listens, you're off the hook! The other people have been warned what to expect.

Speaking the truth isn't always easy. Pointing out the enemy (Satan) and his entrapments (sin) won't make you very popular with anyone who doesn't want to hear any warnings of any kind! But keeping quiet and blaming yourself won't help you or your friends if something truly terrible happens. So be watchful and be warned! As God leads you into a deeper awareness of spiritual matters, tell others who need to know.

PRAYER: Dear God, it's hard enough to be aware of dangers myself without having to worry about other people! I know that I'm responsible for my own decisions, and other people are responsible for theirs. But if I see something that I know will hurt them or get them into trouble, please give me the conviction, courage, and compassion to speak out boldly so they can hear. Give me the words and the love. In Jesus' name.

JOURNALING WITH GOD: Is God urging you to speak to a friend about something you know is harmful?

_____

_____

_____

_____

DAY 49

The Lord is my shepherd,
I shall not be in want.
(Ps. 23:1, NIV)

Sometime during the first few weeks of college, there's a possibility you'll run out of money! The financial aid department may take a while to process your loans. Your on-campus job may hold your check until the first week of the following month. Your bank account may be overdrawn, and your meal ticket may cover less than your appetite!

Unless your parents happen to be on campus, it's pretty hard to hit them up for a couple of dollars now and then. You could phone, but you don't really want a lecture about balancing checkbooks. Besides, you were feeling good about handling everything yourself and now it's, well, embarrassing to be caught short.

Before you pour your woes onto your roommate or someone else who's known to have a thick wallet, you should probably know that most students get themselves into this predicament. When it comes to money, you're not unique! You just need a little more practice at balancing figures and making cash stretch—first to cover necessities and then to cover wants.

Most likely, though, you're not as destitute as you feel. You may have plenty of wants, but that doesn't make you "in want." Even if you're presently impoverished below the penny level, that doesn't make you indigent. You have a dorm roof over your head and a payday coming soon! So confess any misappropriation of funds to God, your Shepherd, and seek His guidance. He will protect you from lack and lead you as you need.

PRAYER: Dear God, thank You for taking care of my needs. I haven't always made wise decisions about the funds that my parents, school, or campus job contributed for my education and support. Forgive me for treating money as something I expect to be there whenever I want or need it. Only You are always there for me! Thank You, Lord, for being my Provider as I follow You. In Jesus' name.

JOURNALING WITH GOD: Discuss your needs with God.

_____

_____

_____

_____

_____

_____

_____

Let no debt remain outstanding,
except the continuing debt
to love one another.
(*Rom. 13:8, NIV*)

Is it payback time? Sometimes you may feel you have no choice but to borrow money from your roommate or another dormmate so you can get by until your next check comes. Although borrowing can usually be avoided, crunches typically occur as part of most college educations!

When you encounter these situations, however, the way you handle the first no-cash episode can set a pattern for your thoughts, actions, habits, and expectations for the future. For example, you may find yourself expecting people to loan you money each time you put your hand out. Or you may expect them to ask you each time to pay them back—hoping, of course, they'll just forget!

God's Word sets another standard. On behalf of the person(s) who loaned you money, He asks you to pay it back as soon as you can. The repayment of a debt depends on available cash, though, not feelings. If it were left to how you feel, you'd probably rather spend the monies on something you want that's new instead of a loan payment that's old!

Paying back what you owe may empty your pockets again. But like everything He requires, God has His reasons. For one thing, He wants you to look to Him as your Provider. For another, an outstanding debt makes you indebted to someone other than Him, and God wants no one to have a financial hold on you!

As your Provider, God asks you to pay up quickly so you won't be called into account by anyone but Him. He asks you to owe nothing but love—the long-overdue debt of sin Christ cancelled from the cross. That's the one loan payment you're perfectly free to spend and spend and spend!

PRAYER: Holy Father, Giver of all life and love, thank You for providing me with Your good gifts. Help me to pay what I owe and be indebted to no one but You. Thank You for Your Son, who cancelled my debt of sin and credited my account as paid in full! Help me to draw each day from Your affluent love. In Jesus' name.

JOURNALING WITH GOD: Ask God to help you recall and repay what you owe.

A good name
is rather to be chosen
than great riches,
and loving favor
rather than silver and gold.
(Prov. 22:1, KJV)

Did you know that your ability to borrow involves good credit? You probably won't have to fill out an application to get your roommate to loan you a fresh pair of jeans. You may only need to give your name and student number to check out a book from the campus library. You might even get a small loan from a friend simply by holding out your hand or saying, "Please." But in each of those instances, you'll receive credit for your own good name. Your name becomes collateral—the bargaining power worth more than the money needed to cover a new pair of jeans, a new book, or a new loan.

Without signing anything, however, do you know you place your good name on the line each time you borrow something? It's like having credit without the hassle of paper or charge cards! This privilege shows you're good for anything that's been temporarily loaned to you.

When you promptly return what you borrow and quickly repay what you owe, you enhance your credit record. You show credibility. You let people know you can be trusted to return books to the library or money to a friend or clothes to your roommate. Instead of tossing any of the above items beneath the bed and forgetting about them, you show regard for people who were kind enough to loan you what you needed. You also show regard for your own name. But most importantly, your prompt repayment of anything you've borrowed brings honor to God's name and principles. This gives Him the credit when your credit is due!

PRAYER: Dear God, forgive me for the times I've delayed in returning what I've borrowed. Help me to repay what's due as quickly as possible. I choose a good name—my own and Yours. In Jesus' name.

JOURNALING WITH GOD: Talk with God about anything you've felt that He, your parents, or another person owes you.

_____

_____

_____

_____

_____

_____

_____

_____

_____

*Pay to all
what is due them.*
(Rom. 13:7, NRSV)

Did you return the phone call from that message your roommate left on your desk the other night? Did you repay a visit to the person down the hall who keeps dropping by to see if you're in your room? Do you owe someone a letter?

Paying what's due doesn't necessarily involve material things or money. It also involves your time. Oh, it's not that anyone has the right to keep tabs on your private time or make claims on your personal interests. But your family, old friends, and dorm neighbors do have a legitimate request: They just want to hear from you! Either their love, blood tie, or proximity gives them that right.

With your first semester at college well underway, you may already be feeling pressured by everything you have to do. That's to be expected as you learn to juggle insufficient hours in a day! If the pressure continues to increase, you may even find you need to drop a class before the withdrawal period ends. Or perhaps you need to cut an extra-curricular activity for a while.

Be careful, though, about dropping friends or cutting family ties. People need each other—at home and church and in the dorm. Everyone needs to belong, to fit in, to be a welcomed, valued part of a neighborhood, family, or group. So even if you aren't feeling particularly close to anyone right now, remind yourself that feelings do change. New bonds will be made. Closeness can occur.

In the meantime, old friends, new friends, and family have offered to loan you their priceless attention! Honoring that debt may require a commodity you've already found is scarcer than money—time! However, you don't have to spend hours writing letters or chatting with someone. Nor do you need to tell everyone how very busy you are! As you consider what's due, tell what's new! Then repay simple interest for interest.

PRAYER: Heavenly Father, thank You for giving me people who care about me and are willing to give me their attention and time. Help me to have a realistic schedule to maintain my studies and my relationships with other people—and You. In Jesus' name.

JOURNALING WITH GOD: Talk with God about your use of the time He has loaned you.

_____

_____

_____

_____

_____

Pay to all what is due them—
taxes to whom taxes are due,
revenue to whom revenue is due,
respect to whom respect is due,
honor to whom honor is due.
(Rom. 13:7, NRSV)

Have you discovered that you don't like all of your professors equally well? Some may seem too eccentric or too cerebral or too full of themselves! Others may be pleasant enough or nice enough, but rather boring. Still others may have an unusual, entertaining, or highly convincing way of making their subject matter important to you.

Like everyone, college professors are just people who need sleep, meals, and occasional fresh air. Some may be annoying to be around; others may be delightful company to keep. But regardless of their pleasing—or displeasing—personalities, you owe each of your instructors something that only you can give.

What? Well, that depends! If you find a subject taxing, you may owe a professor those taxes on your time or interest! If you haven't yet paid your tuition, you may owe the revenue or income your instructors receive for doing a job. And even if you don't like a subject—or the person who teaches it—you owe your professors respect for their time. You also owe the honor due them in their field of expertise.

That may be especially hard to pay if an instructor has been causing you grief, confusing your wits, or lowering your

GPA! But all that's owed isn't lost! You can always honor that person regularly with your prayers, and then see what happens! Either the professor will change or your interest will! Meanwhile, your over-taxed gray matter will reap good revenues because you've chosen to obey your one true Teacher—God.

PRAYER: Heavenly Father, You know one of my professors is driving me nuts, so I guess You know why it's happening. I sure don't! Please work this out, Lord. Please heal whatever makes this person so abrasive or obtuse, unkind or just plain boring! Please help me to concentrate on the study material and really hear and understand what's said, not only in this class but in all of my subjects. Help them make sense to me. In Jesus' name.

JOURNALING WITH GOD: Bring your professors to God in prayer. Then listen to His Word to you concerning each.

_____

_____

_____

_____

_____

_____

_____

*One who is slack in work
is close kin to a vandal.*
(*Prov. 18:9*, NRSV)

Since your arrival at college, has anyone's car, dorm, or classroom been vandalized? Such things do occur, especially if a seedy area immediately surrounds the campus. Usually, though, vandalism does not result from a neighborhood's lack of financial worth, but its lack of self-worth.

Impoverished people who take pride in doing *what* they can as *well* as they can would not dream of trashing someone else's possessions! However, persons who don't care about anything or anybody may try to wreck what others have. Since this destruction begins not by acts of vandalism, but by attitudes of worthlessness, such persons are particularly in need of prayer.

As you pray for vandals and the prevention of vandalism, thank God that you're worth a lot to Him and He to you! Then take care not to slack off in your studies or lay waste the reasons that you're there. Don't let emotional distractions or destructive attitudes ruin your college days!

Ask yourself if you're letting other people's chronic problems or unnecessary interruptions invade your study time. Are you telling yourself that, as a Christian, you just *have* to help people who feel worthless about themselves? Do you feel guilty if you don't give full attention to someone who seems to need all of your attention all of your time? Do you think you have to do something to alleviate every problem that every dormmate has? You don't! You can't! Such help and healing come only from God!

Your part is to pray, and then proceed with your own work. Otherwise, you may be slacking off and allowing vandalism of your time, your emotions, your concentration and, ultimately, your education. In college and other neighborhoods of life, you'll find the need to set limits on yourself and on the intrusions of other people. So check your borders for vandalism, and keep anything worthless from wrecking your health, your emotions, and your education.

PRAYER: Dear God, being a Christian is confusing! I know You want me to be helpful, kind, and loving to other people. Yet I see that some problems go too deep for me to fill the lack. Thank You, Lord, for being worthy to take on every concern that everyone brings to me. Help me to let go of the false guilts and false expectations I place on myself or others. Protect me from the physical and emotional vandals against my time, concentration, and energy. Help me know where to draw the line between problems that are Yours alone and those that are mine. In Jesus' name.

JOURNALING WITH GOD: Consider who or what is wrecking your work or study time and give those concerns to God.

So do not worry about tomorrow,
for tomorrow will bring
worries of its own.
Today's trouble
is enough for today.
(Matt. 6:34, NRSV)

Do you know one of the major differences between college students who succeed and those who fail? Pace. Instead of racing at full speed until they drop or lagging until they quit, successful students move steadily ahead. How? They see a goal, aim for it, and do what they can to get a little closer each day.

Aiming toward a goal can be difficult if you're unsure about a career, but don't let yourself worry about that now! Instead, let college graduation itself be your objective. By the time you reach your junior or senior year, you'll have a better idea of what you'd like to do. By then, you will have acquired new information about your interests and your career possibilities. You'll also have lots of practice in learning to trust God to lead you and to help you set a proper pace.

Meanwhile, just concentrate on today. For example, ask yourself if you've put off an assignment, hoping it won't be noticed in your grade. Have you found yourself caring less about a subject that doesn't entice you? Or, have you felt that you're so busy and trying so hard that you cannot afford to spend another moment on something you don't immediately understand? Has your aim been to give 100 percent of yourself 100 percent of the time so your energy level—and grades—just don't add up if something unexpected is required? Have you often wondered where the day went or had to tell yourself, "I'll take care of that tomorrow"?

If so, you may need to reconsider your schedule and routines. Then you can make adjustments so you're not pushed to your outer limits. How? Seek and find a steady, unhurried pace where you can realistically complete today's work today. Tomorrow's work will then fall into place tomorrow because by then, it'll be today!

PRAYER: Dear God, it's hard to find a healthy balance between overwork and procrastination! Please help me to be realistic about the things I'm to do right now. Help me to succeed in doing them without worrying about tomorrow. Keep me on a steady pace. In Jesus' name.

JOURNALING WITH GOD: Ask God for His reality check about the expectations you're placing on yourself and on your time.

_____

_____

_____

_____

_____

_____

*The sleep of a laborer
is sweet.*
(Eccl. 5:12, NIV)

Are you having trouble sleeping? Do you need ear plugs, fresh sheets, or a foam pad for your bed? Too much noise in the dorm and too many lumps in your mattress probably won't help you rest very well! Neither will too much or too little work.

If you haven't been keeping up with your studies, you may be worrying instead of sleeping. If so, just pick up your pace and sweeten your dreams! However, you may find you have a heavy load you can't do anything to change this semester. If that's the case, you'll need to find ways to turn off your high level of mental activity before you go to bed.

Several things can help. First, make a point of never ever opening a textbook on your bed! By keeping the sleeping quarters of your room off limits for studying, you separate the two areas so one doesn't overlap the other. (Of course, this also means no snoozing at the desk!) Do, however, use your sleeping area to open your Bible and journal each night. God's Word can quieten your thoughts and bring comfort, rest, and strength for a new day.

Before you turn out your light, put every concern out of your mind and onto paper. By making a list of "Things To

Do," you separate mental activities. You'll rest easier knowing that the list will help you remember what needs to be done when you can get to it. Also, you'll place off limits those unproductive thoughts that you can't do anything about in the middle of the night anyway!

Finally, be aware that late night discussions or debates can hinder sleep. Again, just set limits—this time by not talking with your dormmate or other friends about any issues that ruffle your serenity after, say, nine o'clock. However, do talk about anything anytime with God! If you find yourself starting to worry about something, stop right there and pray! Then keep praying until you feel at peace about each concern, knowing that it's in God's hands.

PRAYER: Heavenly Father, it's a good thing You don't need to sleep! Thank You for being ready, around the clock, to talk with me through Your Word and through prayer. In Jesus' name.

JOURNALING WITH GOD: Ask God to show you anything that's been worrying you or hindering your sleep.

But none saith,
Where is God my maker,
who giveth songs in the night?
(Job 35:10, KJV)

Okay, you've gotten a sheet of dimpled foam to make your bed more comfortable. You've asked the people next door to cut down the volume so you can sleep. You've made a list of everything you need to remember for tomorrow. You've read a psalm and the next chapter where you left off in the Gospels. You've prayed and journaled and done everything else you can think of, but instead of rest, you're getting more exercise than you want from all this tossing and turning. Before you work yourself into a lather, try asking if God your Maker is making you awake for a reason!

As a body drifts towards sleep, hidden thoughts have a way of floating up to the surface. You may find the rise of a harbored sin that needs confessing. You may find shells of a broken relationship on the shores of your mind. You may find a wave of remorse, a surge of fear, or a general drift of unforgiveness. Whatever you find hidden, treasure the quiet as you give these collectibles to God.

If, however, you're beached in insomnia with nothing you can really see but your own sandy eyes, God may be making you aware of someone else's prayer need. To find out, just ask: "God, do You want me to pray about something?"

If so, He'll quickly bring a person or situation to your mind. For instance, you may have an impression of a specific prayer or request you're to make, perhaps for a friend's safety. Or maybe you'll feel urged to pray for God to lead someone into a healthy decision. You may feel drawn to claim a Bible promise on a person's behalf.

Whether your wakefulness is for your needs or those of someone else, let God lead you through each concern. Listen as He provides the names, thoughts, or words He wants you to bring to Him in prayer. Then thank Him for giving you these harmonious songs in the night.

PRAYER: Dear Father, You know I'd rather sleep than pray! Yet I thank You for bringing to mind the things I forgot to confess or discuss with You earlier this evening. Thank You for making me part of Your intercessory plan. In Jesus' name.

JOURNALING WITH GOD: Listen to the prayer needs that God puts on your mind.

_____

_____

_____

_____

_____

_____

From then on, whenever
the evil spirit sent by God
came on Saul,
David would get his harp
and play it.
The evil spirit would leave,
and Saul would feel better
and be all right again.
(1 Sam. 16:23, TEV)

Have you noticed how your dormmates have their personal tastes in music? Some like their jazz hot, their rock soft, and their metal heavy. Some listen only to rap, while others think it's about as rhythmic as a leaky faucet. But despite the sounds preferred, if everyone turns up the volume at the same time, the din can be rather dis-concert-ing!

In concert or in private hearing, music has the power to change moods. Not only the "mood music" used with a romantic evening in mind, but every tune can alter its listener's mood or state of mind within just a few seconds! That's right! Not minutes—seconds! Of course, most people don't consider their brand of music as that potent or mind-altering, but in a way, all music is.

Think about it. Have you ever seen a fretful child quieten under the soothing sounds of a lullaby? Have you ever felt blue until someone turned on a lively tune that got you tapping your foot in time to the beat? Have you ever gone from feeling restless in church to feeling happy, just because you got to sing your favorite hymn?

As you select the tape, CD, or song that you'll play on your radio or stereo, be aware that you're playing with power! You can choose to fill your room with lively tunes, happy songs, and soothing symphonies. Your music can bring harmony and good cheer. Your instrumentals can be instrumental in helping troubled listeners be all right again.

PRAYER: Heavenly Father, You know that sometimes I just want music to express what I'm already feeling, but I don't want to impose an off-key mood on anyone else! Help me to be an instrument of Your hope and peace. Help me to stay in tune with You. In Jesus' name.

JOURNALING WITH GOD: Ask God about His sound of music, and be ready to hear!

DAY 59

*It is better to hear
the rebuke of the wise
than to hear
the song of fools.*
(*Eccl. 7:5, NRSV*)

The psalmist understood the power of music and used it effectively to calm the troubled soul of the king. In fact, the very word "psalm" means song. It's no wonder, then, that the same musician's psalms (usually read today instead of sung) have the power to change a person's heart and mind—from despair to hope, disbelief to faith, grief to joy.

As you listen to the music in your dorm, consider its sound—or unsound—effects! Make a point of really hearing the lyrics in your favorite songs. Think about whether or not they help you to express what you think, feel, or believe to be true. Notice if the impact helps to uplift, strengthen, and encourage the people who hear.

Songs have the power to build up a listener, but they also have the ability to tear down and destroy. The music in your dorm could be promoting violence, discord, or rebellion. It could be setting people's nerves, tempers, and teeth on edge. It could be filling the air with sounds of foolishness.

The Bible says it's better to have a wise person scold you than to have to listen to foolish words or foolish songs! Words of wisdom have the ability to sink deeply into the spirit, but useless, irrational, and senseless words do too! They too can

118

sink into a low, subconscious level, making the hearers fool-ishly think ill of themselves, their lives, other people, or God. Music usually has either a good or a bad effect on its listeners. Songs can minister help and healing or hurt and harm. The beat can pulsate comfort or work people into a frenzied pitch! The words can lift or lower moods.

As you surround yourself with the sounds of music, use its power wisely. Create a melodious environment that helps you to study well, sleep well, and think well of God, self, and other people!

PRAYER: Heavenly Father, help me to sing praises of You! Guide me to choose music that's pleasing to You and benefi-cial to me and my dormmates. In Jesus' name.

JOURNALING WITH GOD: Talk with God about how different types of music affect you.

_____

_____

_____

_____

_____

_____

_____

I am the Lord your God,
You shall have
no other gods before me.
(Ex. 20:2–3, NIV)

One hazard of college life is having so many demands on your time and attention that it's easy to forget about God! Your education, studies, and new relationships demand a lot from you, but you still have to take family and old friends into account too.

God wants you to love other people. He wants you to like your school, His gifts, and what you're doing with them. He wants you to love yourself. However, He doesn't want you to worship anyone but Him, serve anyone but Christ, or be led by anyone but His own Holy Spirit.

As you balance your busy schedule and maintain your relationships, stop occasionally and ask yourself what or whom you're serving. What or whom are you following? What or whom do you simply adore?

Ask, too, if your decisions are based on pleasing God or pleasing people. Do your words, deeds, and actions speak well of Christ and your name, Christian? Have you sung praise of God in your heart, kept loving thoughts of Him in your mind, and put your body in the presence of His people? If you honestly doubt it, you may need to rearrange your priorities and perhaps loyalties—not only to the Lord but to

His bride, the church. By keeping company with the company of Christ, you'll find it's harder to forget God and His good gifts to you. If others are in this with you, though, you'll find that you're more apt to worship, serve, and adore only Him—not just on Sunday mornings, but throughout each week of your life.

PRAYER: Dear God, only You know how very many things are on my mind. Only You know the fears, doubts, and concerns I have—not to mention the attractions and distractions! Only You (well, maybe my folks and roommate!) know how hard it is for me to get up on Sunday mornings. So, Lord, I need Your help! Draw me into the company of Your people. Help me to follow You more closely. Help me to worship, serve, and adore only You. In Jesus' name.

JOURNALING WITH GOD: Ask God to reveal to you anything or anyone you've placed before Him.

_____

_____

_____

_____

_____

_____

_____

I am the Lord;
that is my name!
I will not give my glory
to another
or my praise to idols.
(Isa. 42:8, NIV)

Has anyone knocked on your dorm door or called you on the phone when you weren't sure who was there? Depending on the tone of the speaker, you may have felt anything from puzzlement to alarm. But before you let the person in or went on talking, you probably asked, "Who is this?" or "Who's there?" Then, you found out what the person wanted.

God doesn't leave people guessing! Before He speaks, He clearly identifies Himself. He makes no argument for His own existence. But He does say straight out who He is, so there won't be any doubt about it. He also says why He's calling, so there's no doubt about that either. He says: "I AM the Lord," and He lets you know exactly what He wants—for you to bring praise, honor, and glory *only* to Him.

Sometimes that's harder than it sounds! Sometimes it's easier to praise a CD that's just been released or honor a stack of charge cards with unlimited credit! It's definitely more popular to idolize a sexy movie star or glorify the skill of a well-known athlete than to give thanksgiving and praise to God. But are you giving credit to some*one* or some*thing* for what God Himself has done?

For example, when a person applauds your gifts, do you

point to God as Giver? When you talk about how you got to college, do you credit God for having opened the way for you to come? When people thank you for something you've done, do you let them know you wouldn't have done anything to help if God had not put it on your mind and given you the ability?

People cannot keep quiet when they applaud! If they're excited or glad or thankful about something—whether it's winning a ball game or getting a new sweater on sale—they can't help but tell their good news. So whenever you tell others your really good news, just be sure to mention God's name.

PRAYER: Dear God, forgive me for taking You for granted! Forgive me for taking credit or giving it to others when it was due only You. Thank You, Lord, for being worthy of all praise. Help me to honor and glorify You. In Jesus' name.

JOURNALING WITH GOD: Ask God to help you recall the blessings from Him.

_____

_____

_____

_____

_____

_____

*Don't let your people
practice divination
or look for omens
or use spells or charms,
and don't let them
consult the spirits of the dead.*
(Deut. 18:10–11, TEV)

Isn't it exciting to see students from all over the country—and other countries too—strolling across your campus? Learning about other regions and cultures can be fascinating, especially when people tell about the customs and traditions they brought from home.

As you get to know students from around the country and around the world, however, you'll soon discover a need to be careful not to offend people who don't automatically know where you're coming from. Since you weren't brought up in the same places, you can't always guess what's okay with a person and what isn't. For instance, what's considered a fad in your area could be silly or old hat or even offensive to some people and downright insulting to others!

The bigger surprise, though, is that some students might shock you! For example, to people from most sections of the United States, a charm bracelet just means a pretty piece of jewelry. But to students from areas who practice voodoo, those cute little bangles are also called a "fetish" and are meant to charm away evil spirits. (Yeah, that's how it got its name.)

Other peoples from other cultures may evoke the names of

gods you didn't know existed. They may even try to carry on a real live conversation with real dead people! With a medium and cooperative ancestors, they might even believe they succeeded. So don't be surprised by such practices! But do not be in awe!

God didn't say other gods do not exist. He warned: Stay away from them! No matter how fascinating they seem, they'll only bring you harm. Only God Almighty is pure love, merciful justice, and real truth. Only He has power to save, forgive, restore, and redeem.

PRAYER: Lord God, thank You for Your almighty power at work in my life! I call on You and only You. In Jesus' holy name.

JOURNALING WITH GOD: Think about the character and nature of the living God.

In the land
*   you are about to occupy,*
people follow the advice
*   of those who practice divination*
*   and look for omens,*
but the Lord your God
*   does not allow you to do this.*
(*Deut. 18:14, TEV*)

Come on! Tell the truth. Have you occasionally peeked at your horoscope in the newspaper? Have you ever wished upon a star? Have you seen a falling star and taken that as a good omen?

Star-studying (astronomy) and star-searching (astrology) look at the same sky, but take different pictures! On campus, you'll probably see both. Usually, you will find astronomy students to be mathematically inclined persons who like to calculate the distance from one star or planet to another. Sometimes they have scientific or specialized interests in observing matter, meteors, or weather patterns. Although they draw intellectual conclusions about the night sky, astronomy students are often reminded of how small they are and how infinite, almighty, and astronomically great is the Creator of the universe.

Astrologers search the sky for other reasons. They look for omens and trends to help them predict the future. They misuse the God-given signs of the changing seasons as indications of who or what people are—signs that answer wonders about what each astrological group should be or do. Then they cast horoscopes to tell these people how to live their lives.

126

In the dorm, you'll discover people who read horoscopes now and then and think nothing of it. Other dormmates won't do anything without seeing their horoscope forecast for the day! They may ask what your sign is, and if it's not compatible with theirs, they'll cast your friendship aside!

Whether it's done a little or a lot, reading horoscopes is a way of seeking guidance from celestial bodies. Even if readers try to take the prediction lightly, a forecast is good for casting them into a tizzy or holding them hostage! How? They're looking for what is bound to happen!

Only the unchanging God can free you from entrapments of the past. Only He can protect you in the present. Only He knows the way to guide your future for all eternity.

PRAYER: Heavenly Father—Creator of all the universe—forgive me for seeking signs when I wonder about my future. Forgive me for looking to anyone but You for answers about who I am and what I'm to do. Thank You, Father. Praise You, Lord, for guiding me safely and steadily toward Your light and love. In Jesus' name.

JOURNALING WITH GOD: Consider God's ways of guiding you.

_____

_____

_____

_____

_____

By your lies
you discourage good people, whom I
do not wish to hurt. You prevent evil
people from giving up evil
and saving their lives.
So now your false visions and mislead-
ing predictions are over.
I am rescuing my people from your
power, so that you will know that
I am the Lord.
(Ezek. 13:22–23, TEV)

Have you ever wished people would just tell you what you want to hear? That's the appeal of fortune tellers, palm readers, psychics, and spiritualists. They may have different "reading matter"—i.e., tea leaves, crystals, tarot cards, brain waves, tone of voice on a telephone, or lines on a hand. Yet each is a line meant to snag you, reel you in, and keep you hooked on seeking their advice!

Do they advise you from the kindness of their heart? Do they have your well-being in mind? No, they have a hand on your wallet! College students who are seeking directions for their studies, careers, or future mates make especially good prey! By hooking into common fears about the future, these "advisors" keep people coming back, again and again, to pay for the daily question, "What should I do now?"

God, of course, is the only One whom you should ask about your present choices or future goals. But although He is unchanging, God is not always predictable! He may require something in return—something harder to pay than money—something that is not at all what you want to hear! He may say no when you want a yes. He may say wait when you want to hear, "Now!" He may tell you to change something you don't want to change before you can expect lasting results. Regardless of how He handles each situation, you can always trust this: God speaks only truth. He has only your truly best interests at heart. He doesn't have to "read" you! He knows you! He made you. And He understands you and your needs better than anything in heaven or anyone on earth—better than you even know yourself.

PRAYER: Lord God, You alone can be trusted to know what's truly best for me. Please help me to hear and obey Your good direction for me. In Christ's name.

JOURNALING WITH GOD: Ask God to help you hear what He's been trying to tell you.

As Jesus was sitting
on the Mount of Olives,
the disciples came to him privately.
"Tell us," they said,
"when will this happen,
and what will be the sign
of your coming
and of the end of the age?"
(Matt. 24:3, NIV)

Even Jesus' disciples wanted to know about the future! They asked when certain things would happen and what signs would clearly show the end of the age. In answering, Jesus did not specify when. However, He did tell what to expect—not to predict present trends or future possibilities—but to prepare His present and future followers for hardships, while strengthening faith in the one true God who knows all.

In your dorm, you'll find people who think they know it all! They believe human beings control their own destinies—if they just put their minds to it! They believe a utopia or ideal world will be reached when people are more enlightened, better educated and have their consciousness raised to higher and higher levels. They believe in themselves and their own human potential, rather than God.

It's interesting to note that special music (often a primordial sound) accompanies these beliefs. Yet students are not the only ones listening. Otherwise intelligent people, such as college professors, may also be professing a New Age.

If such bright people cannot see clearly, how can you? Well, by yourself, you can't! But remember, Jesus told His followers (including you) what to expect! He specifically warned of "false christs." Obviously, that includes souls, but really sneaky false christs would also set themselves up as saviors of the land, the seas, the ozone, the environment—and human nature too.

In the meantime, the Rock of Ages has not lost strength! Upon that sturdy, steady Rock stands the church, and the age of the church—Christ's bride—has not been disclosed! The age to come has yet to come, and when it does, guess what? There still won't be a New Age! There will be the reign of the ageless, eternal Messiah—Jesus Christ your Lord.

PRAYER: Holy Father, this New Age stuff is so insidious, it's hard to recognize. I didn't realize that people were putting themselves higher than You! Thank You for bringing down high places that exalt human nature, intellects, or egos! Thank You for giving me discernment and revealing to me all I need to know as I need to know it. And, Lord, frankly I'm glad that saving souls and the whole earth does not depend on me, but You! Help me to know exactly how You want me to help. In Christ's name.

JOURNALING WITH GOD: Ask God for discernment and talk frankly with Him about anything that's been confusing you.

_____

_____

_____

_____

_____

The idols speak deceit,
diviners see visions that lie;
they tell dreams that are false,
they give comfort in vain.
Therefore the people wander
like sheep oppressed
for lack of a shepherd.
(Zech. 10:2, NIV)

As you get to know the people in your dorm and in your classes, you usually tell them where you're from, don't you? Maybe you talk about your family and the long-term interests you've had, such as hobbies, sports, or art. To know these dormmates and classmates better, you'll eventually ask about their background and interests too.

As a friendship builds, you'll probably swap stories about exciting vacations, special achievements, or traumatic events. Most likely, you'll tell one another highlights from your lives so you can get to know each other well. By sharing information and feelings, you gradually begin to understand each other's future goals and dreams.

Friendship with God works in much the same way. By seeing what He's done in the past, you get a clearer picture of what He plans for the future. By learning the background of His people and how they came into being, you get a better idea of where He's leading them now. Without such information or shared feelings, however, you're apt to come to the wrong conclusions! Often, that's just how cults get started.

Have you noticed how self-proclaimed prophets begin and end with Revelation? If they know anything at all of the

Hebrew Testament, it usually comes from Daniel—the other apocalyptic book about the end times. Maybe they'll toss in other Scriptures to spice what they say, but the main course is futuristic and often feeds people's misconceptions or fears!

Instead of gathering false impressions about the one true God, just open His family album regularly. Begin reading at the beginning and go on until the end. By doing that, you will get a clearer picture of who and what God is. You will also gain a closer Friend.

PRAYER: Dear God, help me to get to know You better. Help me not to take Your Word out of its whole context. In Jesus' holy name.

JOURNALING WITH GOD: Ask God to reveal any misconceptions you have about Him.

_____

_____

_____

_____

_____

_____

_____

Therefore, there is now
no condemnation
for those who are in
Christ Jesus,
because through Christ Jesus
the law of the Spirit of life
set me free from the
law of sin and death.
(Rom. 8:1–2, NIV)

Have you run into anyone yet on campus who believes in reincarnation? Did you feel, well, uncomfortable in hearing about this view but uncertain of what you were to say? Did you remain quiet in hopes the problem would not reincarnate itself?

As you get to know God and His Word more and more, you will feel easier about dealing with spiritual confrontations. That's what you're up against when you combat misconceptions about religious truths. Since most college students wonder about God and actively seek answers to their questions about spiritual matters, you may encounter lots of combat!

To help you handle these weighty matters, God promises to give wisdom to those who ask. Often this becomes apparent as you suddenly know what you're to say. You may have such an inspired answer that you're pretty sure you didn't think of it by yourself!

Another way God gives wisdom is by helping you recall the very Scripture that answers well what you've been asked. He may quicken specific Bible verses or general Bible truths, bringing them to your mind right when you need a particular word. Or He may help you discern an error in other people's thinking as they tell you their beliefs.

Whether a spiritual confrontation involves New Age, humanism, satanism, cults, reincarnation, or anything else, a single truth says what all people need to hear: Only Jesus Christ saves sinners from sin.

People may deny sin, but no one can avoid it! No one but Christ can redeem. No one but the Lord can forgive. No one but He has the power to save you for eternal life—not just in some future time, but in your life right now!

Because of the incarnation of God's Word in Christ, no one needs to be reincarnated. No one has to repeat a life—or a mistake—again and again in hopes of getting it right the next time! God got it right through the life, death, and resurrection of His Son! Therefore, you are not condemned! You are forgiven! And you're given a new beginning in each new moment of each new day.

PRAYER: Heavenly Father, help me to be clear in my heart, mind, and spirit about Who You are so I can clearly know and tell others. Thank You for Your love, truth, wisdom, mercy, and forgiveness. Praise You for having power and authority to give such good and perfect gifts. In Jesus' name.

JOURNALING WITH GOD: Ask the one true and holy God about your need for a Savior. Consider how your act of confession and His act of forgiveness in Christ perfect you every day.

_____

_____

*Jesus answered them,
"You are wrong,
because you know
neither the scriptures
nor the power of God."*
(Matt. 22:29, NRSV)

On your campus or in your dorm, you'll probably find as many religious beliefs as you do shoe sizes! Some sound like a tight fit. Others seem to fall apart because they're so loosely structured or poorly connected! But this isn't just true of other religions. Very likely, you'll find a varied assortment of spiritual sizes and conditions within the main denominations of the Christian faith too.

Jesus ran across this problem in the religious community of His day. Some people believed in life after death. Some didn't. But both groups managed to try on biblical truths and occasionally squeeze them to fit in a way they liked best. Both groups liked what felt comfy and familiar to them.

This still happens today for the very same reasons Jesus stated: (1) Christians do not know the Bible very well; and (2) they do not recognize the power of God at work in their lives or in the lives of other people.

How does this happen? Sometimes a church misdirects its members by not regularly teaching Bible stories in church school or by not directly reading the Bible in every worship service. At other times, a denomination misshapes biblical doctrine or erroneously applies Scripture to say what most of its members want to hear. For instance, a group may avoid mentioning Jesus as personal Lord and Savior because they don't understand what that means and feel uncomfortable by it. Or a church may confuse an aspect of the distinctive, ongoing work of the Holy Spirit, making Him seem no larger than the individual use of one of His gifts.

To avoid being misshapen, place your faith only in God—Father, Son, and Holy Spirit. Fit your faith to His Word—the only fit source of spiritual truth. Believe in His power—the only fit means of shaping, healing, and protecting people's lives. Then look for the greatness of His acts and the magnitude of His work—work that He has miraculously fit into His church—and you!

PRAYER: Thank You, Lord, that from the moment You saved me into eternal life, You began to shape me to a new life in You. Help me to seek You each day as Master of my decisions and actions. Help me to know well the Scriptures and the power of God at work. In Jesus' name.

JOURNALING WITH GOD: Consider the power of God and His incarnate Word in Christ.

_____

_____

_____

_____

_____

But to all who received him,
who believed in his name,
he gave power to become
children of God.
(John 1:12, NRSV)

As you get to know Christians on campus who come from other denominations, you may discover conflicting thoughts within the church. You may need to search the Scriptures, perhaps using a concordance to look up a specific topic, to settle a matter within your own mind. You might also want to tell other Christians the biblical truths you have found—if they're willing to listen and if you're willing to leave the results up to God!

As you become more familiar with God's Word, His power, and the other denominations who are represented on campus, it's fairly easy to find a whole lot to argue about! But please, don't. Christians are to be known by their love—not their ability to debate!

You can, of course, state the reasons for your personal beliefs or conclusions any time you feel led to do so. But the perfect word and timing needed to set people straight is a job of the Holy Spirit! He is the One who guides and leads God's people into all truth.

So instead of squabbling about spiritual matters, focus on who and what matters: God sent His only Son into the world—not to condemn the world, but that the world, through Him, might be saved. If, therefore, Christ did not come to condemn, neither should the Christians who go by His name! That's not to say you won't disagree with people or think they're wrong. They very well may be! Just remember, Jesus said they're wrong because (1) they don't know the Bible, or (2) they don't know the power of God.

Other Christians need your prayer—and need you to be aware: They're God's children too! Because they do believe and have received Christ into their lives, they also have the power that comes from being in the immediate family of the one true, holy, and living God.

PRAYER: Dear God, forgive me for bad-mouthing the church or Your children! I'm sorry, Lord. I need to judge for myself what's true, but now I see that judgment means coming to a verdict about the truth. It doesn't mean sentencing those who haven't yet fully decided what is true! Help Your children, including me, to see clear evidence of You and Your Word. In the loving testimony and living name of Jesus.

JOURNALING WITH GOD: List the names of brothers and sisters in Christ whom you believe God wants you to keep in prayer. Then pray for each as the Holy Spirit leads you.

DAY 70

*For all who are led
by the Spirit of God
are children of God.*
(Rom. 8:14, NRSV)

Isn't it wonderful? God sent His Holy Spirit to stay with you in college! This isn't just an overnight guest, though. God's Spirit accompanies you to classes, to the campus library, back to your dorm, and wherever you need to go. You're not being followed! But how can you know you're being led? Simple! You have God's mind and spirit—His perspective—instead of your own!

If you're reading God's "instruction manual"—the Bible—you can be sure that those guidelines have you in mind! So you can trust God's Word to bring a word to you as needed.

God may also direct you through an inner knowing and an outer circumstance. If, for instance, He has something He wants you to do, He will give you a sense of peace about it and even arrange what's needed to enable you to obey.

As you seek God's direction about an action or decision, He will guide you through Scripture, inner peace, and outer conditions. All three of these directional indicators need to agree with one another. If you take one by itself, you could be misled! Say, for example, your roommate wants you to go to a hangout for Christian students called The Ark. Instead of looking to see if conditions are favorable for an outing or asking God to give you peace about what you're to do, you close your eyes, open your Bible, and point to 1 Chronicles 13:10, "The Lord's anger burned against Uzzah, and he struck him down because he had put his hand on the ark" (NIV). To follow that lead alone would be more like reading a fortune cookie than the Bible! If, however, you see that verse when your friend can't go after all and you felt uneasy anyway, maybe God wants you to stay out of that place!

God doesn't mislead His children, but they might mistake the route! Like any wise and loving parent, He wants you to stop, look, and listen to His signals. Then you can proceed in confidence, knowing that He has you in hand through all of the spiritual traffic and intersections you encounter. If He sees you're in danger—spiritually, physically, emotionally—you can be sure He'll try to tell you! However, if you're not paying enough attention to His directional indicators, it may take a stronger nudge of uneasiness, a sharper word from His Word, or a really loud circumstance to get you to hear and heed!

PRAYER: Heavenly Father, I don't want to be hard of hearing, seeing, or knowing! Thank You that You can be trusted to lead me straight to where You want me to go. Thank You for always being my true, steady, and dependable Guide. Help me to follow Your lead more closely. In Jesus' name.

JOURNALING WITH GOD: Ask God to show you any area of your life or your relationships where you've taken the lead away from Him.

_____

_____

Now that you're well into the first semester of college, you've already faced many new temptations and decisions. In the days ahead, you may have more alternatives to choose from—some obvious and some difficult to discern. You know God is leading, but you may wonder if you're following! How can you be sure you're on the right track?

Bible truths and commandments, such as the Beatitudes and the Golden Rule, will guide your general direction, of course. But through His Word, will, and ways, God also speaks to individuals individually.

As you listen to the inner knowing or peace within you, you'll learn to hear before you take the next step. Then if you feel uneasy, you can accept that as a reminder to stop and pray and listen more! It could be that you're feeling afraid and simply need to recognize that before you proceed. Or it could be that you're to go another route.

Either way, God will guide you if you let Him. He might even ask other people to give you His word! If your parents are Christians, they're His likely choice. After all, they have a good idea of who you are and where you're headed.

Your parents may also know tendencies in you that you

haven't yet figured out—or ones you'd prefer not to see! For instance, they may be aware that you often take things too seriously—or too lightly—so maybe they're already praying that neither trait will affect your studies. Or maybe they have cautioned you about a particular friendship. Or maybe they just want you to be more careful about going out late at night or across a dark campus alone.

You're not in grade school! You don't have to listen! But no matter how independent you are or how far away your parents live, you will always be their child. You can obey them in the Lord. Their loving Christian counsel about a complex situation or confusing choice may be God's way of guiding you toward the direction that's just right for you.

PRAYER: Heavenly Father, I don't want to have to run to my parents with every decision! I need to hear You myself. But Lord, when I'm uncertain, please remind me to seek Christian counsel from my parents or other family members who know and love You—and know and love me. In Jesus' name.

JOURNALING WITH GOD: Talk with God about concerns where you have no clear direction.

_____

_____

_____

_____

*"Honor your father and mother"—
which is the first commandment
with a promise—
"that it may go well with you
and that you may enjoy long life
on the earth."*

(Eph. 6:2–3, NIV. See also Deut. 5:16.)

Have you called your parents lately or written them a note? Have you realized that it's to your advantage to keep in touch—not to touch them up for a few more dollars, but so you can hear your mom or dad's voice and alleviate some of the homesickness that you feel?

Unless you were an absolutely rotten, incorrigible kid during every minute of your childhood, your parents really do miss you! Unless you've had a totally pathetic or completely depraved childhood, you miss them too. But even if your whole family has not always been kind to one another, God did not say it's okay to dishonor parents who've acted dishonorably! He didn't make His command relative to their actions. He made it dependent on yours!

Can you relate to the word "honor" and have some idea of how that's to be translated into your actions today? Honoring your father, mother—and grandparents too—means showing them respect, courteously regarding what they say, and giving them a measure of consideration. Honoring them also gives them credit for having brought you into the world and doing what they could to provide for your needs.

If they failed, honoring them means forgiving too. Maybe

they haven't changed one bit. Maybe they truly don't deserve much from you. But as you forgive your parents for every awful, atrocious, colossal, and teeny tiny mistake they have made, you're free to be at ease instead of dis-ease about the past. You're free to be well and live long in the family of Christ.

As you honor your parents, you will keep in touch—not just with them, but with God too. Honoring your parents gives your obedience to God, and that brings the blessing, glory, and honor due His name as the heavenly Father of all.

PRAYER: Holy Father, praise You for being worthy of all honor and respect. Praise You for Your holiness. Thank You for Your forgiving love—not only for me, but through me to my parents for their mistakes, large or small. Help me, Lord, to show them Your love always. In Christ's name.

JOURNALING WITH GOD: Ask God to remove the sting from any hurtful childhood memories. Ask Him to bring His healing light to each situation you recall.

"For I, the Lord your God,
am a jealous God,
punishing . . .
for the sin of the fathers
to the third and fourth generation
of those who hate me,
but showing love
to a thousand generations
of those who love me
and keep my commandments."
(Ex. 20:5–6, NIV)

Have you met your roommate's parents yet or gone home for the weekend with someone from your dorm? After watching the family interact for a while, did you notice how much your friend takes after one parent or another? Could you tell if someone in that family—or yours—has passed on a talent, a mutual interest, or an unhealthy habit? Your great-grandparents might have referred to someone's "good or bad blood." Your grandparents might have discussed "history repeating itself." Your parents might have mentioned character traits that you or another family member inherited. But whatever phrase people used, they really meant the "sins of the fathers revisited upon the children."

If you've heard that expression yourself, you may feel doomed to some weird genetic imprint that you can't possibly correct! For instance, if no one in your family has ever graduated from college, you may feel you don't have a prayer! Or if everyone goes to grad school and beyond, you may think you're "programmed" (today's way of putting it) to stay in college for the rest of your life!

Like most misconceptions, this one has a basis of truth. And the truth is: People really are doomed to bad blood, historical repeats, character flaws, genetic imprints, or dysfunctions in one's programming *if* they hate God and refuse to let His healing love transform their lives!

Fortunately, though, the often-quoted passage from Exodus does not end where most people stop reading! It goes on to tell how God's love continues for at least a thousand generations, bringing blessing and freedom to those who love and obey Him.

You can't do anything to change your ancestry or the choices of past generations. But you can choose to trust, love, and obey God so that—through Christ—His pure family bloodline cleanses yours! As you accept His transfusion of love and forgiveness into your life, you can then receive God's regeneration for yourself and for countless generations yet to come.

PRAYER: Praise You, Heavenly Father, for freeing me and my family from the mistakes of generations past—as well as the sins of this day. Help me not to become entrapped again by old habits, but to seek and find Your way for me. In Jesus' name.

JOURNALING WITH GOD: If you haven't already done so, begin a healthy habit of giving your family—and your concerns about them—to God.

_____

_____

_____

_____

He shall take him
to the door or the doorpost
and pierce his ear with an awl.
Then he will be
his servant for life.
(Ex. 21:6, NIV)

Have you had your ears pierced? You may have done that many years ago. Or depending upon your background, your parents may have made that decision before you were old enough to remember. When parents express disapproval of this popular practice, though, some people just wait until they're away at college before they run and have it done. Or they may wait to get a dozen or more pierces up and down each lobe! Either way, the idea is apparently *not* to have one's ear pierced by loud objections of *"why* did you do *that?"*

Ear-piercing is a matter of personal taste or cultural influence. But pierced ears are also shot through with a symbolism of slavery! Obviously that isn't what you had in mind! But God did—and for a very particular reason.

In Hebrew culture, impoverished people sometimes became the bond servants of other, more well-to-do folks for seven years. When this temporary arrangement ended, the servants had to decide if they wanted to go free, and take care of themselves, or if they wanted to remain in someone else's keeping as a slave forever.

Then, as now, some people did choose to be enslaved. For

whatever reasons they had at the time, they agreed to remain in the custody of their owners. This agreement, however, was permanent and binding. If the person later regretted the decision, that was too bad! A pierced ear marked the slave as someone else's property in much the same way that the ear of an animal might be tagged today!

Even if you didn't realize the significance of having your ears pierced before you did it, your choice doesn't have to be permanent and binding. You can choose to stop wearing an earring (or any other piece of jewelry) that marks you as a slave to something that's symbolized by the design. Or, now that you know, you can be glad you found out! You can let your earrings and other jewelry act as a permanent and binding reminder that you have dedicated yourself to Christ and asked Him to be the Lord and Master of your life forever!

PRAYER: Dear Lord, thank You for being Lord! Sometimes I'm not exactly sure what that means, but I want to place myself into Your custody. Thank You for wanting that too! Thank You for refusing to enslave me and for giving me the freedom to choose to love and serve You. Praise You for being the one Lord and Master I can fully trust to protect me, provide for me, and lead me. In Christ's name.

JOURNALING WITH GOD: Talk with God about His job descriptions for you as His servant and Himself as your loving Lord and Master.

_____

_____

_____

DAY 75

As you enter the house, greet it.
If the house is worthy,
  let your peace come upon it;
but if it is not worthy,
  let your peace return to you.

(Matt. 10:12–13, NRSV)

The first time you make a trip home from school, you'll probably see some changes that have occurred while you were gone. The decor may have been altered. A younger sibling may have grown taller. Family interests or concerns may have focused elsewhere. Or maybe nothing is out of place, but everything seems different!

Most likely, you're the one who has changed! At first glance, nothing may seem familiar, even if it's stayed exactly the same. Why? Having been away awhle, you cannot help but look at your family and house differently—perhaps more objectively than you were able to see them when you lived there every day.

As you look at your mother or father, for instance, you may suddenly see them as individuals—people with a life of their own apart from yours. That can be a jolt! Yet it can be enlightening too as you really notice your mom's smile or your dad's corny sense of humor or the seriousness with which either of them performs a certain task.

If tensions exist, you may also notice that! You may find yourself wishing that one or more family members would lighten up or learn to express their emotions in a positive, nonthreatening way. You may wish you could hurry the weekend and get back to the dorm where you now feel more at home!

Regardless of your situation, the family's residence and the people there are still your home. For your sake, their sake, and the sake of the Lord, you need to wish it well!

Before you even walk through the door, speak a word of peace to family members and to the house itself! Greet them with Christ's love. Give God's blessing to your neighborhood, your house, and your family. Let His peace reside, and as it does, you'll be more at home again.

PRAYER: Dear God, thank You for giving me a home in You. Thank You for my family and the place where they live. God, bless my parents and every member of this household. Let no ill will have hold of me or anyone! God, bless this house and my being here. In Jesus' name.

JOURNALING WITH GOD: Discuss with God what He would have you do to bring His peace to your family household.

_____

_____

_____

_____

_____

_____

Whoever loves a brother
or sister
lives in the light,
and in such a person
there is no cause for stumbling.
(1 John 2:10, NRSV)

While you've been away at college, has a younger brother or sister taken over your room? Seeing that change when you go home to visit can be pretty upsetting! You may feel as though you've been shoved out the door—permanently! But even if your bedroom still belongs to you, you may get the impression that someone in the house has been messing with your stuff!

So, what if they have? What are your options? Well, you could puncture a lower lip, trying to keep quiet. You could make a federal case and court the favor of the parent who's most likely to give the verdict you want. You could buy a padlock and bolt your bedroom door.

Instead of taking any of those choices, why not take your case before the Lord? Ask Him to help you talk with the person in a way that would be helpful to that family member and correct the problem too. Ask Him to help you express your feelings without passing sentence on the one who invaded your territory. Then listen to the thoughts that come.

For instance, you may see that having the contents of your room rearranged doesn't bother you nearly as much as having to face yet another unexpected change. Or you may see that something you left behind means more to you than you thought, so now you know to take it back to your dorm. You may see that a younger sibling—or a parent—has taken over your room because of something they themselves need. Or you may see that no one meant to fill your former space but just wanted to bring you closer again.

As the Lord places your thoughts and feelings in His light, you'll also see what He wants in this situation! He wants you to bring His peace into your home, say what truly needs to be said, and show His love to the brother, sister, and other family members whom He has given to you.

PRAYER: Dear Heavenly Father, thank You for being with me through all the changes I've had to face in going away to college. I miss familiar places and my home, but I guess my family misses me too. Help me not to react from emotions, but to respond to Your love for my family. In Jesus' name.

JOURNALING WITH GOD: Talk with God about the changes you see at home, in your family, or in yourself.

DAY 77

*Some friendships
do not last,
but some friends
are more loyal than brothers.*
(Prov. 18:24, TEV)

If your family has lived in the same town or community for a while, you probably have friends you want to see when you go home to visit. That's great—assuming, of course, that these people also want to see you!

Some won't! Others will, but they may not be available. That's another change you'll face—an end to the days when you could get together with high school chums without giving it much effort. Realizing this can be a shock at first, but a scattering of people can also be a blessing! Since it's no longer a simple matter to get together with old friends, your true friends will be easier to see. If you phone unexpectedly or pop by someone's house when the person didn't know you'd be in town, naturally you won't catch everyone at home. That's okay! But you might ask yourself why you didn't let that friend know you were coming. Were you calling out of habit instead of a genuine desire to see the person? If so, that's okay too, but you need to be aware that this friendship may not mean as much to you as you once thought!

Sometimes the proximity of people within a neighborhood, church, or school creates a closeness based on the location—not on the closeness of the people. Now that may be happening in your dorm as students get together because of shared space rather than shared interests. The dormitory itself creates a common bond as people come to that place with friendliness, but not necessarily in friendship.

Friendly attitudes come first, of course. Then, with enough attention on both sides, that friendliness may take root and develop into a hearty relationship, whereas lack of interest will stunt its growth.

As you see this important distinction—at home or church and away at school—you will be able to discern the difference. Then you can distinguish the real friendly people from the real people friends!

PRAYER: Thank You, Lord, for the friends you've given me in the past, present, and future. Bless each one, and help me to discern the true friends from those who are just being friendly. Help me to be a friend to others in Christ.

JOURNALING WITH GOD: Talk with God about what's valuable to Him in close friendships.

_____

_____

_____

_____

_____

_____

Then Jesus said to his disciples,
"If anyone would come after me,
he must deny himself
and take up his cross
and follow me."
(Matt. 16:24, NIV)

During your visit home, did you locate old friends and make plans to get together? If so, you may feel annoyed that you have to check with your parents before you go out! After being on campus for several weeks, coming and going as you please, you may not have expected to find your old curfew still standing!

If you're tempted to cut restrictions, keep in mind that home life differs from dorm life. Your parents, grandparents, siblings, or others in your house have their sleep patterns, work schedule, and activities to consider too. It may disturb them to have you coming and going at odd hours. Or perhaps emotional disruptions would occur as younger family members bring their restrictions into question.

Parents and others in authority have a responsibility to give their ruling on a matter in order to maintain discipline and help the entire household function well. So if a ruling makes you feel cross, take up that crossness! Deny yourself the right to argue crossly, be at cross purposes, or cross-question your parents! Follow their lead and be a disciple.

That's what a disciple is—a follower. However, the job of a leader is to keep followers in line and on track—considering individuals while regarding the whole group. Discipline permits this. Discipline makes disciples. Whether or not house rules make sense to you, they've been made for a reason. Instead of setting yourself at odds, consider yourself as one who follows Christ. Then look to His lead. Accept the discipline to which Jesus submitted Himself as He became a disciple, not of His own wants and wishes, but of His Father's will.

PRAYER: Dear Heavenly Father, when I've heard those words about denying myself and taking up a cross, I thought it meant I had to deny my feelings or who I am and become some kind of a martyr! Now I see that You want me to stop trying to lead my parents or You! Forgive me for breaking step by not following the lead of authorities You have placed over me. Help me to be disciplined well as Your disciple. Help me to keep in line with Your will for the church and Your way for me, individually. In Christ's name.

JOURNALING WITH GOD: Ask God to bring to mind any times you denied how you felt or who you are. Ask Him to show you the value of accepting your self-worth in Him and the value of denying any self-centeredness that makes you out of step with His lead.

_____

_____

_____

_____

*Whoever does not have the Spirit
cannot receive the gifts
that come from God's Spirit.
Such a person
really does not understand them...
because their value can be judged
only on a spiritual basis.*
(1 Cor. 2:14, TEV)

Maybe you haven't noticed the changes, but you've been maturing these past few weeks! You're learning how to be on your own. You're learning the necessity of self-discipline to get any work done! You're learning to draw closer to God. Any of those changes can produce an immediate—and perhaps opposite—effect on family members or childhood friends! Their reaction may be strong enough to alter your relationship—temporarily or for a very long time.

Why? With these important changes, common bonds have changed too. For example, your family has had to adapt to your being in another location. Your friends who don't take education seriously have had to adapt to the fact that you do. Your changing level of spiritual maturity sets you apart from those who do not want to hear about God.

Knowing this can help you understand what's happening as a formerly close friend or relative pulls further and further away. As much as it hurts, this distancing isn't personal! Well, actually it may be! It could be a personal rejection—not of you, but of the God whom you serve.

As you come to see that a non-Christian cannot understand spiritual matters, you then know what to do: Pray for the person. Show Christ-like love to the person. And wait for God to move the person! Until that happens, you can expect even an old friendship to fade.

Why? Nothing on earth separates two people more than having one of them love God and the other hate Him or be disinterested! However, nothing on earth brings two people closer than a relationship found and bound in the living Christ.

PRAYER: Dear God, when people I love pull away, I feel as though someone has died! Is that how You felt when the disciples denied You and fled? Is that how You feel when I pull away? Forgive me, Lord. Draw me near You and bring me into close fellowship with other people. In Christ's name.

JOURNALING WITH GOD: Pray regularly for family members or old friends who suddenly seem distant. Ask God how He'd have you respond to each person in each situation.

_____

_____

_____

_____

_____

_____

_____

If your campus isn't very far away, friends from your hometown may have chosen the same college you did. As these old friends—and new friends from your dorm—adapt to life on campus, you may begin to notice changes in them. Some will be for the better. Some will be for worse. Some will be so awful, you'll wonder if you ever knew the person at all!

Maybe you didn't! Even if you've known people from your earliest childhood, you may never have had the opportunity to see how they would react to the choices and temptations they now face—especially since their parents aren't looking over their shoulders every day! As you look back, though, you may realize that these changes have been coming for a long time. If so, you may need to back off from the relationship.

Why? Why would you want to give up on a friend—even temporarily? If you sense that someone has been given over to a depraved, ungodly mind, you may need to step out of the way. For one thing, you don't need companions who pull you down or increase the temptations you encounter! For another, you'll have very little in common with people who shut God completely from their lives.

You also don't know what God knows is needed to get through to a person. If you continue to hang around, you could hinder Him from working freely. How? If, for His own reasons, God must withdraw from someone, your presence brings His presence back onto the scene! God cannot abandon you! He promised He wouldn't leave those who seek Him. Yet He may remove Himself from those who continuously refuse Him.

If you see this happening, let God be God. Work with Him by giving Him room to do His job, and then do your part by keeping your friend in prayer.

PRAYER: Dear God, thank You for being with me and giving me the discernment I need. I can't imagine how awful it would be to have to live without You, even for a little while! I don't want my friend to go through that either, but I trust You to know what's best. Please put on my heart and mind the very prayers that you would have me pray. In Jesus' name.

JOURNALING WITH GOD: Listen and note what comes to your mind about how you're to pray specifically for your friend.

_____

_____

_____

_____

_____

*So I tell you this,
and insist on it in the Lord,
that you must no longer live
as the Gentiles do,
in the futility of their thinking.*
(Eph. 4:17, NIV)

Old friends and new situations on campus will probably give you a lot to pray about! So will new information as you study and learn from professors who don't always know the Lord. You may find you have little choice but to walk away from friends, standards, or ideals that deny God. At other times, you may find that staying will make a difference!

The difference you make depends in part on holding this biblical word in mind: Don't live like a non-Christian; don't allow futile thoughts. Actually, those exhortations overlap one another because action begins with thought. If people think a certain way, eventually they'll act accordingly.

Since so many types of people live and work on campus, you'll run into all sorts of futile thoughts! For instance, one person may have delusions about his own self-importance while another has absolutely no belief whatsoever in his God-given abilities. Futile thoughts may be petty ones that make people focus on nitpicking complaints about other students, professors, or themselves. But futile thoughts can also be so all-encompassing that they entertain every worthless idea that comes along!

To help you recognize futile thoughts in general, look for

ones which serve no useful purpose. They may be largely ineffectual—or so small they're frivolous! Either way, futile thoughts are fruitless ones. They accomplish nothing productive. They produce nothing helpful, useful, loving, good, or kind.

As you listen to the opinions of your professors, dormmates, or other people, God can help you discern what's worth learning, keeping, and using—and what isn't! You may also see that your own opinion has been telling you something that doesn't help a bit! Done long enough, and you may be living in the futility of your thinking. But don't wonder! Find out! Ask God to reveal any futile thoughts that block His perfect will and productive way for you.

PRAYER: Heavenly Father, I confess that I've been letting my doubts about myself or someone else get in the way of who I am and what I'm to do. Help me not to have empty thoughts, words, or actions. Help me to be productive in my studies, relationships, abilities, and use of time. Thank You for leading me into a fruitful life. In Jesus' name.

JOURNALING WITH GOD: Ask God to reveal any futile thoughts or actions you've had. Ask Him to show you how to be more productive.

_____

_____

_____

_____

Finally, beloved,
whatever is true,
whatever is honorable,
whatever is just,
whatever is pure,
whatever is pleasing,
whatever is commendable,
if there is any excellence
and if there is anything
worthy of praise,
think about these things.
(Phil. 4:8, NRSV)

Since futile thoughts are worthless, have you wondered what thoughts are worth keeping? The NRSV Bible lists several worthwhile possibilities, including whatever is true, just, pure, pleasing, commendable, excellent, and praise-worthy. KJV includes whatever is lovely and of good report. NIV says to think about whatever is noble, admirable, or right.

Thinking about such wonderful things doesn't sound too hard. But by now, you could probably write a book on the campus oddities you've seen, heard, or thought! Peculiar preferences may have caught your attention in the dorm while distressing facts may have given you food for thought in your classes. Disturbing thoughts about international turmoil or your own inner, emotional turmoils may have kept you awake, while boring information may have put you to sleep!

No doubt, you could write a book about what you've already seen and learned, but why not let God write His Word in you? As you decide to take note of whatever is good, true or lovely, He'll help bring such thoughts to your attention. He'll help you read yourself better—and better comprehend circumstances around you! He'll translate futile, negative thoughts into a positive course of action.

How does this happen? As you think about whatever is true, you'll incorporate that truth into your life, instead of acting on false information. As you think about whatever is excellent in the instruction you receive, you'll be more apt to want that excellence reflected in your studies. As you think about whatever is pleasing to God, you'll know how to please Him in use of time and talents and the relationships you choose.

PRAYER: Dear God, I've noticed on almost every newscast how bad news comes first—sometimes to the exclusion of anything good! It's depressing to hear. But now I see it's even more depressing to live my life as an ongoing record of bad news! Help me to recast my thoughts so my thinking is in line with Your good will. In Jesus' name.

JOURNALING WITH GOD: Talk with God about the bad news you've been replaying, again and again, in your mind. Note the good news He brings as He helps you to consider whatever is worthy in and around you.

*And be not conformed
to this world:
but be ye transformed
by the renewing of your mind.*
(Rom. 12:2, KJV)

During these first days in college, you may have found you're being re-educated about yourself! As you develop more productive thoughts, feelings, and routines, you may begin to see yourself—perhaps for the first time—in the light of God's will and purpose for you.

So how do you look to yourself? How do your studies, instructors, and friends appear to you? Are you seeing flaws or strengths? Are you examining successes or failures? Are you focusing on what's lamentable or what's worthy of praise—not only in yourself, but in your personal studies, habits, and relationships?

Taking a brief look at negatives can help you to make wiser, healthier, and more positive choices now. Dwelling on old habits or mistakes, though, can keep you bound to regrets—and that's not very productive!

During these first weeks in college, maybe you didn't give enough attention to your studies, and now it's beginning to show in poor grades. Maybe you made a bad decision to accommodate whatever seemed acceptable to your dormmates or other students. Maybe you yielded to chronic pressures or turbulent emotions and used drugs, alcohol, or sex to feel better and then discovered you felt much worse!

Conforming yourself and your standards to those you find around you is not what God wants for you, of course. Yet He knew this would happen! He knew you wouldn't receive an A+ in every test you take. He knows you're not perfect! But Christ is!

By confessing a wrongdoing, you can be assured of God's forgiveness. So accept that! Receive it! Then be careful not to conform to the worldliness around you. Instead, let your mind be transformed. How? As you read the Bible daily, God's thoughts will become yours. His Word has the power to renew, resolve, and transform your thoughts—from futile, fruitless thinking to a creative, productive mind that's at one with Him.

PRAYER: Heavenly Father, I thank You and praise You for your forgiveness! Thank You for the at-one-ment of Your Word made Man in the life, death, and resurrection of Your Son, Jesus Christ. Help me to keep my thoughts at one with Yours by the power and promise of the risen Lord, in whose name I pray.

JOURNALING WITH GOD: Ask God to reveal any thoughts or habits you have that are out of line with His Word.

Finally, be ye all of one mind,
having compassion
one of another.
(1 Pet. 3:8, KJV)

As you let God's Word transform your thoughts and renew your mind, guess what else might happen? You may find other Christians on campus who think a lot like you! That doesn't mean you'll agree on every interpretation of every verse, but you will have the Bible as the primary reference point from which your thoughts and their thoughts come.

The more you read the Bible, the more your thinking will align with God's thoughts and with other people who regularly read His Word. Denominational differences will lessen, and compassion will develop among Christians who know the Bible well—from "In the beginning" to the last "Amen"!

You'll seldom find "one mind" like this in the academic world. Usually, a single reference point doesn't exist. So regardless of the subject, you'll run across numerous experts whose opinions differ. Even factual data that's accepted one day may be discounted the next.

That can be confusing—especially if you have an exam coming up! Your best option then is to look over your study notes and concentrate on understanding the material presented by the instructor, since that's the information on which you will be tested. As you take an exam, you can focus on what's being asked, answering each question as directly as possible.

If you and other students think like your instructor, you'll be of "one mind" and have a grade to prove it! If you try to think like God, you'll begin to see each other's point of view through His. By better understanding what God thinks, you'll be more inclined to share His compassionate thoughts toward other Christians. Then you will find people on campus who think like you, simply because they think like Him.

PRAYER: Dear God, sometimes I hear so many confusing thoughts and so much conflicting information, I don't know what to believe! When I do know, I sometimes feel like I'm the only one who thinks that way! Thank You for giving me the Bible as the source of Your inspired, true, and living Word. Thank You for reminding me that other people want to know what You have to say. Help me to find Christians on campus who think like You. In Jesus' name.

JOURNALING WITH GOD: Discuss with God how to come together with other Christians in His Word.

If we walk in the light,
as he is in the light,
we have fellowship
one with another.
(1 John 1:7, KJV)

In these first days of college, have you sometimes felt in the dark about what was going on? Have you sometimes felt alone? Have you sometimes felt your plans are without shape or void of any real companionship?

In the first days of creation, God said, "Let there be light," and light sprang into being. God called the light "good," and as He continued to create, He called everything else good too. But do you know what finally made God say, "It is not good"?

No, it wasn't sin. In Genesis 2:18 (before sin occurred), God mentioned something else. He said, "It is not good for man to be alone."

Just as surely as God first created light, He created man-kind—male and female—to have fellowship with Him in that light. He also meant for His children to use His light to find companionship with one another.

If you've been feeling in the dark or alone, let God be the illumination you need to find His "helpmeets" for you on campus. He can show you organizations for Christian students that are best suited to your interests and abilities.

For instance, if you're athletically inclined, you may have a lot in common with other Christian athletes. If you like to sing, you may enjoy being part of the campus choir. If you're drawn to learning more about other denominations, you may find your niche in the school's campus ministries. You may prefer to be involved in your denomination's student union on campus, or you may want to participate in activities for young adults at a nearby, local church.

Whatever you decide, don't stay by yourself in a closet! Let there be God's light on the activities and companionships that He says are good for you!

PRAYER: Dear God, You know how I've been feeling! You know how hesitant I've been to get involved in anything besides my studies—or just getting used to being on campus! Yet I see the importance of spending time with other Christians who share interests similar to mine. Please bring Your light to the organization or activity to which I'm well-suited. Help me to find fellowship. In Jesus' name.

JOURNALING WITH GOD: Let God bring to light your interests and abilities. Then ask for His focus on a single group where you're to be involved—at least in the beginning.

_____

_____

_____

_____

_____

DAY 86

*Let your light shine
    before others,
so that they
    may see your good works
    and give glory to your Father
    in heaven.*

(Matt. 5:16, NRSV)

As you ask God about the extra-curricular activities in which He wants you to become involved, He may nudge you in a direction you hadn't expected! His light may suddenly place you in the limelight!

When you think about it, it makes sense that God would prefer having Christian leaders on campus, right? Well, that leader just might be you! Maybe you're to become involved in student government. Maybe God will see that you're in charge of hall activities for your dorm floor. Maybe He'll put it on your mind to start a new group on campus or a Bible study in your dormitory.

God may also place you in a position of leadership within the classroom. He may have you set the pace for a lively discussion. He may ask you to speak up, speak out, or speak with intelligence, conviction, and humor.

Whether God has you address a small class or an assembly of the whole school, you will automatically be in a spotlight. So let your light shine! But instead of basking in that light until your ego glows, remind yourself that God has placed you where other people can readily see not you, but Him.

As your brightness becomes apparent, your leadership

172

position puts you in position to turn the light away from yourself and onto God. That's quite a responsibility! But responsibility means you're able to respond well—to those who follow and to the One who leads. This may be the very reason why God is leading you into leading others! He knows that you're response-able. He knows that He can trust you to be the kind of leader who leads others straight to Him.

PRAYER: Heavenly Father, I really haven't seen myself as a leader on campus, within a class, or in the dorm. Yet I don't want to follow anyone but You! Help me to reflect Your light and lead others toward it. In Christ's name.

JOURNALING WITH GOD: Ask for God's light on the leadership ability and response-ability He's given you.

_____

_____

_____

_____

_____

_____

_____

_____

_____

*A student is not
above his teacher,
nor a servant
above his master.*
(Matt. 10:24, NIV)

On campus, in church, or throughout the world, you'll find that the very best leaders are those who are themselves led by God. In the classroom, the very best students are those who simply allow themselves to be taught!

Most likely, you would have avoided a college that had a terrible reputation in the academic world. Yet even if you aren't fond of a particular instructor or the textbook used, you can still choose to learn new information. You can focus on the highlights of a subject, gather additional resource materials, and get feedback from other students who seem to enjoy the class.

As the time nears for you to register for the courses you'll take next semester, you might also ask other students about specific subjects and the individuals who teach them. You can arrange to meet a professor or request a syllabus for a class you're considering. You can seek the counsel of your college counselor or an instructor whose opinion you value.

Ideally, you'll do best taking subjects you enjoy from professors you respect. But you've probably discovered that isn't always possible! You may get stuck with an instructor you dislike in a course that's required! A class you want may not be scheduled when you're able to attend, or it may have been dropped altogether. Yet, despite the obstacles you encounter, you will learn!

Just as God leads you into what's best for you, so will He provide you with the instruction that you need for the work He's prepared for you to do. He is your leader. He is your instructor. Under His tutelage, you cannot help but be well taught!

PRAYER: Dear God, thank You for providing me with the courses and instructors I need. Help me to follow Your lead and be prepared for all You'd have me do. In Jesus' name.

JOURNALING WITH GOD: Talk with God about the subject matter that matters most to you.

_____

_____

_____

_____

_____

_____

_____

_____

_____

Of making many books
there is no end,
and much study
wearies the body.
(*Eccl. 12:12, NIV*)

Are you getting uptight about your most relaxed courses? Have you been sweating and fretting finals, coming up soon? Do your eyes feel shot from squinting at print? When someone calls your name, do you respond only after taking ample time to consider your answer? If so, you need a break!

How much of a break depends on the load you have been carrying this semester and the amount of time required for you to do the work adequately. If you're carrying a moderate load, you may need to remind yourself at two or three-hour intervals to shake the tension from your tendons. If you have a particularly heavy schedule, you may need to get away from your study area entirely, perhaps by going for a leisurely walk or swim. You may need to spend the better part of the afternoon counting clouds, hoops, goals, or sheep.

The idea is not only to exercise your body, but to put your mind completely to rest on a tennis ball—or anything but a textbook. Then you can return to your work refreshed and better able to concentrate. That's what recreation does. It helps you re-create lost energy and enthusiasm for what you have to do.

Everyone needs a good balance of physical, mental, and

spiritual exercise and rest to keep from getting worn out in any one area. So the more devoted you are to your studies, the more you need a break to avoid burnout. Sadly, the brightest, most academically inclined students may be the very ones who drop out of college at the end of the first or second semester because they're just plain weary of studying night and day and in between!

So if you've been feeling like you've had it, maybe you have! Get educated about the equilibrium needed for a well-balanced body, mind, and spirit! Give yourself a break, and take the break you need!

PRAYER: Dear Heavenly Father, You know I want to do well in school. You know how important it is to me to be here. I don't want to let down my family or myself. But sometimes, Lord, I feel so tired of studying, I don't think I can stand another minute! Help me not to get to that point, but if I do, please let that be a reminder to me to take the break I need. Help me to find a healthy balance—physically, mentally, and spiritually. In Jesus' name.

JOURNALING WITH GOD: Listen as God helps you to recall the physical activities you enjoy and most need to pursue.

_____

_____

_____

_____

DAY
89

*Cast all your anxiety on him
because he cares for you.*
(1 Pet. 5:7, NIV)

As you near the end of your first semester in college, you may be feeling anxious about your grades, finances, or the constraints on your time. You may be uncertain about the courses you're to take or the career which you're to pursue. You may be afraid you can't cut it—academically, socially, or emotionally. But no matter what concerns you have, do not even think about giving up college! Instead, give up all your anxieties by turning them over to God.

It won't always be easy, but you can do it! Your daily practice of talking with God through journaling and prayer will help. So will reading the Bible regularly and claiming scriptural promises as your own. Attending church and finding fellowship on campus will also strengthen you as you surround yourself with the encouragement, presence, and prayers of other Christians.

Just remembering to turn your worries over to God will bring you enormous relief. But that's only half of it! The power for you to let go effectively and trust God completely comes from your faith in knowing He cares for you.

Do you know that? Do you know how much He loves you? God knows exactly who you are! He created you! He forgives you! He redeems you. And furthermore, He enjoys you!

178

The Creator of the universe wants the pleasure of your company. As long as you're here on earth, He will come down to you. He will speak to you clearly in His Word. He will even speak in the situations He allows. He will speak to you within the quietness of your own heart.

Let Him speak and listen! The Lord God calls you by name. He says, "My child, my child, don't you know by now how much I love you? You are mine! Never forget that I AM yours—your strength, your power, your love."

PRAYER: Heavenly Father, I praise You for being the Creator of heaven and earth—and me. Thank You for bringing me into closer fellowship with You. Thank You for giving me the intelligence and opportunity to be in school and on campus. But Lord, sometimes I'm so afraid! I just need You to hold me—and all my worries too. Calm my fears, guide me, and lead me into Your way for me. In Jesus' name.

JOURNALING WITH GOD: List your worries, lift them to God in prayer, then listen to His Word to you about each concern.

_____

_____

_____

_____

_____

_____

*He was praying
in a certain place,
and after he had finished,
one of his disciples said to him,
"Lord, teach us to pray."*
(Luke 11:1, NRSV)

Jesus educated His disciples well! As they followed Him closely, they could hear His teachings, see His work, and sense His power. Even though they didn't always understand what He was doing or why, they knew enough to ask questions! They listened to His explanations, examples, and parables, and they learned.

Today this hasn't changed! Part of your education is knowing when to ask questions—of your instructors, college counselors, parents, fellow students, and God. But how do you know when to ask? Simple! Ask anytime you don't already have an answer—and sometimes when you do! Apparently, Jesus' disciples did not have a clear answer about how they were to pray. They asked, and their Perfect, Wonderful, First and Last Instructor outlined His answer and briefly covered the main points. If you don't already know it (and even if you do), you'll find this heavenly syllabus in Matthew 6 and Luke 11.

Say it. Read it. Personalize it. Every day, you can incorporate your ever-changing concerns into the Lord's Prayer. Doing so will bring you the power, guidance, and answers you need—in these wondrous college years and in the life's work that God has prepared for you. In Christ's name.

PRAYER: Our Father in Heaven, let Your name be holy in my life and in this dorm! Let Your spiritual kingdom come and Your will be done on this campus, in my home, in our country, and in the church throughout the world—just as it is in heaven. Lord, give my roommate, my family, and myself whatever You see that we most need this day. Forgive us for stepping over the boundaries set by You or other people. Help us to forgive those who have trespassed against our standards, hopes, rights or feelings. Lead us not into the temptation of giving up too soon or keeping on too long with our studies, and deliver us from any ill of any kind that stands in our way. And, Father, let all this be done in Your power to bring You glory. In the name of our Lord Jesus Christ who taught us to pray.

JOURNALING WITH GOD: Whether you prefer a loose-leaf notebook or nicely bound diary, begin a new first page in college with your version of the Lord's Prayer. Receive God's guidance and blessing as you continue to note the thoughts and insights He brings to you during your journaling time.

_____

_____

_____

_____

_____